ISSUES IN MARXIST PHILOSOPHY

Volume II

MATERIALISM

MARXIST THEORY AND
CONTEMPORARY CAPITALISM

General Editor: John Mepham

This is a new series of texts of new British books and of translations committed to:
The development of Marxist Theory
The analysis of contemporary capitalism, its tendencies and contradictions
The record of the struggles to which they give rise.

ISSUES IN MARXIST PHILOSOPHY

Volume II
MATERIALISM

EDITED BY
JOHN MEPHAM
AND
DAVID-HILLEL RUBEN

THE HARVESTER PRESS

First published in Great Britain in 1979 by
THE HARVESTER PRESS LIMITED
Publisher : John Spiers
17 Ship Street, Brighton, Sussex, England

© The Harvester Press Limited, 1979

British Library Cataloguing in Publication Data

Issues in Marxist philosophy. – (Marxist theory
  and contemporary capitalism).
  Vol. 2: Materialism
  1. Communism
  I. Mepham, John, b. 1938   II. Ruben,
  David-Hillel   III. Series
  335.4′11   HX56

  ISBN 0–85527–706–8
  ISBN 0–85527–726–2   Pbk

Photosetting by Thomson Press (India) Ltd., New Delhi
and printed in Great Britain by
Redwood Burn Limited, Trowbridge and Esher

Contents

Notes on Authors: Volume II

WAL SUCHTING has taught for a number of years at the University of Sydney, first in the Department of Philosophy and then in the Department of General Philosophy, after the split in the former on political-academic issues, at the end of a protracted struggle in which he was active. Since a period, too long, and best forgotten, of 'straight' philosophy, he has been teaching, since 1971, various courses in Marxist studies such as Introductory Marxism, Marxism and Epistemology and *Capital*. He has published in these areas and is continuing work in them. He has been a member of the Communist Party of Australia, a Trotskyist group, and the Australian Labour Party, but is at present unaffiliated. He has been described, by enemies, as an Althusserian anarchist.

ANDREW COLLIER was born in London 1944. He studied philosophy at Bedford College and University College, London. He has taught philosophy at the Universities of Warwick and Sussex and is at present Lecturer in Philosophy at University College of North Wales, Bangor. His main philosophical interests are in issues raised by the human sciences, and in particular by the theories of Marx and Freud. He has published articles in *Radical Philosophy* and is author of *R. D. Laing: The Philosophy and Politics of Psychotherapy* (1977). He has been a member of the International Socialists and the Socialist Workers' Party since 1973.

KATE SOPER is 35 and lives in Brighton. She is preparing a book on Marxism and the Theory of Needs. She was educated at Oxford University and has until recently been a research student at Sussex University. She works as a translator and part-time teacher of philosophy at Sussex University and at the Polytechnic of North London.

TED BENTON worked as a science teacher in a comprehensive school and then studied philosophy at the University

vii

of Leicester and at Oxford. Since 1970 he has taught in the Department of Sociology at the University of Essex. He is an active Trades Unionist and socialist. He has been an editor of and contributor to *Radical Philosophy* and has also published articles in *Studies in History and Philosophy of Science* and *Sociological Review*. He is author of *Philosophical Foundations of the Three Sociologies* (1977).

GEOFFREY HELLMAN studied at Harvard and at Brandeis University. Since 1972 he has been Assistant Professor of Philosophy at Indiana University. He has published articles in *Philosophy of Science, The Journal of Philosophy, Erkenntnis* and other journals.

General Introduction

THE essays in these Volumes on issues in Marxist philosophy are all by authors from English-speaking countries. With only three exceptions, they are printed here for the first time. In these countries, Marxist philosophers have had to struggle over the years, reading and evaluating the works of important continental European philosophers, both Marxists and non-Marxists, and questioning our own distance from them. We have asked what specific contributions our relations to various English-speaking philosophical traditions can make to the advancement of Marxist philosophy, philosophical traditions to which we are essentially related even when the character of that relation is in many fundamental ways a critical one. Much Marxist philosophical writing in the English-speaking world over the last decade has been more or less confined to exegesis and assimilation of continental philosophical systems; Sartre and the Frankfurt School, Lukacs and Korsch, Gramsci and della Volpe, and more recently Althusser, Colletti, and Timpanaro. It will be clear to the reader of these present Volumes that these philosophers have exerted an important influence on their contents. The essays are not written in defiant ignorance or xenophobic dismissal of their work; on the contrary, we respect them by our attention to what they can teach us and by an attempt to make our own distinctive contribution to Marxist philosophy.

Thus, we think the time is ripe for going beyond the rather passive assimilation of continental European philosophy that has hitherto dominated the Marxist intellectual landscape in the English-speaking world. Many English-speaking philosophers are ready to make their own contributions in areas of philosophical discussion in which, in spite of the volume of writing produced by French, German, and Italian Marxist philosophers, debate is still in the utmost confusion. Many of us have the sense that the philosophical argument has not been nearly deep enough, has not made sufficiently deep contact with the really fundamental philosophical issues, and the Marxist positions on central philosophical issues are still quite crude and superficial. Very often, argument and discussion have not been pursued at a sufficiently abstract level, or with sufficient persistence and tenacity. Sometimes Marxist philosophers write as if they must select one of a small number of possible answers to some central issue or difficulty, without exploring all the possible options or alternatives. Marxist philosophy can only advance if it reaches down to the most general and abstract of philosophical categories, by the methods of sustained, persistent discussion and rational argument. English-speaking philosophers have a distinctive role to play here and we hope that this Volume of essays will show this.

These essays are not written by a group of philosophers who in any sense constitute a school setting up a new system of doctrine, a new catechism of truths, let alone reviving any old ones, although they are all written from within a classical Marxist orientation. Two of the essays were written more or less directly under the influence of Althusser, although they are very selective in what they take from his work and are not at all expositions of Althusserian positions. In many of the other essays, the figures of Althusser, Lukacs, Colletti, and Timpanaro appear as worthy opponents, and an attempt is made to open up discussion in a way that is distinctive and which draws more on the English-speaking philosophical virtues of disciplined argument and attention to detailed elaboration and defence of one's own positions.

Overall, a certain coherence of direction emerges from the essays. The reader will notice, first, the persistent appearance of realist categories (potentiality, natural or physical necessity, natural kinds, essence and appearance), some of which derive from the Aristotelian tradition, and all of which indicate, negatively, the deeply non-empiricist or non-positivist ontology and epistemology that dominates these volumes. Marxist philosophy, since its inception, has been driven between the Scylla of positivism and the Charbydis of idealism (usually of a 'humanist' variety). On the one side were figures such as Plekhanov, Engels, Dietzgen, Lenin, Bogdanov, and many writers of the period of the Second

International; on the other, stood Lukacs, Deborin, the
Frankfurt School, Korsch, Sartre, and various 'humanist'
Marxist tendencies. Some, from the Austro-Marxists to
Colletti, could think of no better way out of this impasse than
the slogan 'back to Kant'. Now, there is no doubt that, with
the passage of time, some of the specific concepts or doctrines
propounded in these pages may be found to be problematic,
or untrue to any authentic Marxism, in ways now hidden
from their authors. What is distinctive in these essays, though,
is the attempt to think through a Marxist philosophy in which
Marxism is neither collapsed into a variety of positivism,
nor into a version of idealism, nor is reduced to a footnote to
The Critique of Pure Reason. Whatever historically limited
validity any specific set of doctrines or ideas herein propounded may possess, these essays are important in a much less
limited way for the authentic Marxism towards which they
attempt to move. They do not try to wed Marxism to
current intellectual fashion. They do not say that Marxism
is 'really' Hegelian, or Kantian, or Aristotelian, or structura-
list, or humanist. Marxism is distinctive, and these essays
are distinctive just insofar as they attempt to characterize
that distinctiveness. In most of the essays, empiricism is the
main enemy, but this anti-empiricism is based on a serious
examination of ontological questions which is rooted in
different categories from the currently fashionable anti-
empiricist Marxism of Althusser, or Colletti or Timpanaro.
There is an insistence that the problems of defining dialectical
materialist thought and method can only be undertaken
seriously by an examination of the ontological categories of
physical necessity and *via* an elimination of the empiricist
notion of causality.

A related common theme is the insistence on the need for a
re-emphasis of the importance of materialism and on the
necessity for a realist theory of science. The work of Roy
Bhaskar (*A Realist Theory of Science*, 1975 and 1978) has been
very influential in this area of discussion and we hope that one
of the effects of these books might be to encourage the development of Marxist philosophy in directions which his work, as
well as recent work by Ted Benton (*Philosophical Foundation
of the Three Sociologies*, 1977) and Russell Keat and John

Urry (*Social Theory as Science*, 1975), have opened up. In both these first two common lines of development, there is also a realist insistence by many of the authors on how absolutely crucial it is to distinguish between ontology and epistemology. So much of the confusion and the unacceptable philosophical implications of recent British Althusserian writing can be traced back to the absence of this distinction, or to the inadequacy with which it is worked through. Indeed, some of that writing is naïve enough to pose the explicit abandonment of epistemology, or ontology, or both. Many of the essays in these volumes single out the work of what we might call the British post-Althusserian idealists (especially Hindess and Hirst) as targets for attack, for their work is regarded as, at one and the same time, rather influential and philosophically extremely confused. In this sense, these volumes can be seen as an attempt to intervene in the general Marxist philosophical culture, especially of Britain and Australia, in an effort negatively to combat a specific, dominant, influential body of work and more positively to open up lines of research which we believe will prove much more useful.

Another feature of Marxist theoretical culture which requires critical attention is a certain common style of polemical writing. All too often, much of Marxist theoretical discussion has been marked by the method of 'impugning your opponent's credentials'. Frequently, the fixing of labels has replaced rational argument in these ongoing debates. Simply calling one's opponents 'idealist', 'positivist', 'empiricist', 'mechanical materialist', or 'Kantian', is apparently all that is required in order to discredit their views. When all else fails, the accusation of failing to carry on the class struggle in philosophy (something allegedly done by those who do not accept the accuser's favourite version of Marxism) proves to be a sure winner. Much of the responsibility for this style of argument can be attributed to those Marxist philosophers whose work is insufficiently flexible and undogmatic. Indeed, it is the inflexibility and lack of openness of their views at any one time which leads to the subsequent recantations and auto-critiques rather than the organic growth and development of their positions. Whether intentionally or not, this gives rise to little bands of disciples whose function is to memorize slogans as answers to questions of which they in fact have very little understanding. In the hands of such people, Marxist philosophy has seemed closed rather than open, rigid rather than alive and changing. Among such disciples, especially those of British Althusserianism, abstract, critical thought has often been replaced by complicated technical jargon, whose effect has been numbing rather than the stimulation of clear, precise argument, free from inflexibility, rigidity, and dogmatism. Pat phrases and well-rehearsed slogans have prevailed; repetition and textual exegesis have become the hallmarks of a tradition no longer alive because no longer critical of itself. Each disciple followed his master in every new twist and turn from Marxism and back again, through every period of auto-critique. One could even learn slogans to explain why previous slogans were now to be considered erroneous. Without ceasing to be polemical in the best sense, these present essays are attempts at rational, argumentative, critical thought; they attempt to arrive at justified and well-supported conclusions by the method of Marx and Engels themselves, the method of critical analysis and argument, open to the possibilities of its own fallibility and limitations. In brief, these essays display that undogmatic and flexible character that has always characterized Marxist thinking at its best.

Two more remarks seem in order in this general introduction to these volumes. First, we hope that they will be read not only by philosophers but also by the many Marxists and non-Marxists who are troubled by the questions that are dealt with here. For example, many economists, engaged in difficult discussions about the concept of value and its status, have sensed the need for philosophical literature on the underlying problems of dialectical method and the theory of science. Many biologists and psychologists find that questions about the *materiality* of the objects of their study are directly raised by their own scientific work, and we hope that they will find the essays on materialism helpful. In general, questions of a philosophical character are raised from within very many kinds of intellectual work and practice, and we hope that the majority of these essays will be of use outside the boundaries of academic philosophy departments. More-over, since in the English-speaking world at least dominant modes of thought tend to be empiricist and pragmatic in character, we hope that these essays will link up with an alternative theoretical tradition, available to the workers' movement, which already exists in some areas of intellectual work other than philosophy, which speaks in the voices and accents of the cultural environment of that movement, and upon which that movement might draw in its struggle against capital. Hence, here as always, Marxist philosophy is a philosophy which is itself a political practice.

Secondly, it should already be clear from what we have said that the message of these volumes is not a triumphalist one: we do not believe that the authors have produced definitive solutions to the questions they discuss. These are not books of doctrines in search of disciples. Not only are there substantial differences of opinion among the various authors, but there is also in most of the essays a general tentativeness of tone, by and large a sense of modesty about what has been achieved, and an agreement on the need to recognize the fact that Marxist philosophy, in spite of its age, is still very far from having established even the outlines of a settled and confident adult form on many major issues.

John Mepham
David-Hillel Ruben

Introduction to the Second Volume

EVERY discussion of Marx's materialism must ultimately be based on an effort to distinguish his position from eighteenth-century reductive materialism and from the post-Hegelian materialism of Feuerbach. A new book by Georges Labica, *Marxism and the Status of Philosophy* (forthcoming, Harvester Press), provides a detailed account of Marx's 'exit from German philosophy', with an unparalleled close study of those texts in which Marx and Engels struggled to free themselves from the weight of these earlier philosophical traditions. Labica gives an indispensible and unrivalled historical, biographical and textual analysis of, for example, *The Holy Family*, *The Jewish Question* and *The German Ideology*. What was long needed was a new translation and careful commentary of one of the key texts of this period, the famous *Theses on Feuerbach*, to which every student of Marx must turn, but which because of its brevity, its cryptic formulations and difficulty of interpretation has given rise to endless controversy. In this volume there is a meticulous new translation of the 'Theses' by Wal Suchting together with his 'Notes Towards a Commentary', and these should provide an indispensible point of departure for any future study of this text. As Suchting points out, 'the central theme of the "Theses" is *materialism*. More specifically they outline a critique of "all materialism up to now"'. The study of the development and content of Marx's materialism could have no better starting point than this new translation and notes.

A major figure in stimulating discussion about Marx's materialism in recent years has been Sebastiano Timpanaro whose *On Materialism* (New Left Books) sought to impress on Marxists the importance of taking seriously the limitations and constraints imposed on any human social life by the biological basis of human existence. Both Kate Soper and Andrew Collier in their essays agree with this general position and elaborate its implications. In explaining human poten-tialities and their development it is necessary that historical

I

materialism should in some sense be articulated with other sciences (psychoanalysis, linguistics, biology and so on). Both Collier and Soper endorse a realist and materialist theory of the sciences, and they insist on the need to distinguish between ontological and epistemological materialisms. An enormous amount of confusion has been produced over the generations by the fact that the term 'materialism' has been used in a way that is oblivious to this central distinction. But they also wish to distinguish their own views from those of Timpanaro and to work towards some position which effectively avoids both idealist and reductivist materialist positions. They are stimulated to this by recent debates, especially within the women's movement, about sexuality and sexual differences, and by discussions concerning intelligence testing and race and other controversial issues. The political context and relevance of their thoughts on materialism is abundantly clear, and the originality and subtlety of their views makes their essays essential reading.

Ted Benton's essay is an exemplary study of materialist philosophical texts in their specific historical context of class struggle within culture. Benton seeks to rescue Engels' philosophical works from the ignorant dismissal to which they have been subject for many years, to provide a positive re-evaluation of them which is illustrative of the dynamics of the dissemination of scientific knowledge and the ways in which scientific advances are assimilated by the bourgeoisie. His essay illustrates, with great methodological clarity, the relations between developments in the sciences and ideological struggles within popular culture. In doing this Benton seeks to show that Engels' work contains, contrary to the views of many of his detractors, a non-Hegelian systematic philosophical world-view which is in important respects intellectually defensible. His essay also makes a contribution to one of the main themes of the First Volume of *Issues in Marxist Philosophy*, the much vexed question of the materialist inversion of the Hegelian dialectic.

Finally, Geoffrey Hellman is a more typical representative of the English-speaking analytical tradition in philosophy. His essay attempts to clarify the historical materialist thesis concerning the relation between 'base' and 'superstructure', by developing a rigorous analytic framework of principles of adequacy which any thesis of historical materialism would need to satisfy. He attempts to support the view that 'a core of historical materialism has a coherent, non-trivial formulation, compatible with the full complexity of social systems actually observed while at the same time giving the material base a truly foundational role in the development and transformation of the social world'.

1 Marx's *Theses on Feuerbach:* Notes Towards a Commentary (with a New Translation)
WAL SUCHTING

> Those brief sparks, the *Theses on Feuerbach*, light up every philosopher·who comes near them, but as is well known, a spark dazzles rather than illuminates . . .
>
> Althusser[1]

THE *Theses on Feuerbach*[2] contain some of Marx's most famous utterances. Like *Hamlet* they are 'full of quotations'. Nevertheless it is an extraordinarily difficult text. As Engels said, they are 'notes hurriedly scribbled down for later elaboration, absolutely not intended for publication'.[3] Immensely compressed verbally and in theoretical content, they are written in language heavily loaded with terminology straight out of Hegel, Feuerbach and other predecessors and contemporaries, or with overtones of them. Even more important is the place they occupy in Marx's theoretical development. Written in the spring of 1845, they stand at the point of transition between, on the one hand, Marx's earlier work, in which Feuerbach's thought had a central place,[4] and, on the other, the immediately following production (especially *The German Ideology*) in which he was subjected to a detailed critique and final rejection. As Engels wrote in the same place, they form 'the first document in which is deposited the brilliant germ of the new world outlook'. But only the 'germ': a central difficulty in understanding this text is situating its content accurately, seeing what is new in it without reading back the full wealth of Marx's later work.

Doing this properly would require a large book. Such a book would trace in detail the historical and systematic threads which lead backwards to Marx's earlier work and to what went to constitute this, and forwards to what followed the 'Theses' in Marx's subsequent production. The present

5

piece is not even the sketch of such a work. It is very literally only a set of 'notes towards a commentary', a very rough sketch map whose aim will have been attained if it helps some readers towards a first orientation in Marx's text and enables them to glimpse the intellectual wealth and the coherent unity which is not wholly evident on the surface.[5]

From what has just been said, it is not surprising that all the published English translations (I know of six)[6] are inadequate in various ways. The present notes are based upon a new translation of my own. I am under no illusions about its definitiveness. But if it is just a little better in some respects than has been done so far, that is a step forward and may assist a superior successor. My aim has been maximum fidelity to the original, and deviations from this must be put down to my incompetence rather than to any attempt to make Marx's text more readable in English than it is in German. The translation obviously overlaps with extant versions, both because large parts of the original are very naturally translated in one way, and also because I have simply taken a word or phrase from one or other of them if it suited my purpose.[7]

A Bird's-Eye View of the Theses
To begin with, a rapid glance over the *Theses* as a whole. This will not convey much to anyone not already familiar with them, but may serve to give a general impression which will be useful for situating the subsequent more detailed commentary.

The central theme of the *Theses* is *materialism*. More specifically, they outline a critique of 'all materialism up till now' (Thesis 1), 'the old materialism', from the point of view of 'the new (materialism)' (Thesis 10). Feuerbach's materialism is the particular target, but the criticisms largely go beyond it and are aimed at traditional materialism as a whole. The key to the critique is the idea of 'practice'.

Thesis 1 announces all the main themes to be heard in the rest of the work. Traditional materialism affirms the independent reality of what is other than thought, but fails to take account of the role of human practice, particularly in constituting that objectivity. Thesis 2 goes on to say that practice must be seen as not only contributing to the constitution of objectivity but as the basis of our assessment of the truth or otherwise of our thinking about it. Thesis 3, in the context of a critique of the social theory of 'the old materialism', reverses the emphasis of Thesis 1: here it is affirmed that practice changes not only the 'object' but also the 'subject' of the practice, and indeed that the two changes are simultaneous. Thesis 4 continues the critique of the social theory of traditional materialism, this time in the particular case of the theory of religion – specifically, of Feuerbach's theory. The latter is criticized for failing to see the way in which religion is bound up with a material basis which is (implicitly) a product of certain specific social practices. Thesis 6 continues this theme. (Thesis 5 is essentially only a repetition of part of the content of Thesis 1.) Because Feuerbach does not recognize the primacy of social practices, he locates the origin of religion in isolated human beings. Again because of this he can only site the unity of the species in something common to its members as physical, biological beings. So (Thesis 7) he does not see religion as a social product but rather as something springing from the nature of individual, isolated human beings, the very idea of which is, indeed, the product of a specific form of society. In Thesis 8 the central idea of the discussion specifically of religion in Theses 4, 6, and 7 is stated in general and explicit form: societies are to be conceived as complexes of practices, and mysteries about societies are fathomable by analyzing these practices. Theses 9 and 10 apply this insight to the two forms of materialism which appear in the *Theses* as a whole and which have been introduced already in Thesis 1: each form is the product of a specific form of society. Thesis 11 counterposes in the sharpest fashion the two materialisms: the old, ignoring the role of practice, merely 'interprets' the world, conceived as 'given', whilst the new materialism, based on the idea of practice, involves changing the world.

Now to a more detailed consideration of the individual 'Theses'.

Thesis 1

> The chief deficiency of all materialism up till now (Feuerbach's included) is that objectivity, reality, the sensible world is conceived

only in the form of the *object or of observation*; not however as *sensible human activity, practice*, not from the aspect of the subject. Hence, in opposition to materialism, the *active* side [was] developed in abstract fashion by idealism which naturally does not know of real sensible activity as such. Feuerbach appeals to sensible objects – ones really distinct from thought-objects: but he does not conceive human activity itself as activity *which belongs to the objective world*. Hence in the 'Essence of Christianity' he considers only the theoretical stance as the genuinely human one, whilst practice is conceived and set off only in its grubby Jewish form. Hence he does not grasp the meaning of 'revolutionary', of 'practical-critical' activity.[8]

As was pointed out at the beginning, this first thesis announces, in however muted a form, all of the baisc themes of the text. Specifically, it mentions (somewhat implicitly certainly) the strength of traditional materialism, and (principally) its 'chief deficiency' from the point of view of the form of materialism which Marx is introducing in the *Theses*.[9]

For purposes of analysis and elucidation the thesis may be divided into two parts: the first three sentences and the last two. And of the first three, the first and third are the crucial ones, the second being something of a parenthesis. So let us look in more detail at these two.

Marx says here that the strength of the traditional materialism (Feuerbach's in particular) consists in its affirmation of the reality of a world independent of thought. This strength is more or less taken for granted. But its 'chief deficiency' is that 'objectivity (der Gegenstand), reality (die Wirklichkeit), the sensible world (die Sinnlichkeit[10]) is conceived only in the form of the *object* (*Objekt*) or of *observation* (*Anschauung*); not however as *sensible (sinnlich) human activity, practice*, not from the aspect of the subject (subjektiv)'. Thus, in particular, Feuerbach 'does not conceive human activity itself as activity *which belongs to the objective world* (*gegenstänliche* Tätigkeit)'. Let us look in a little more detail at this 'chief deficiency' of traditional materialism.

The *key* terms here are: 'objectivity' (and 'belongs to the objective world'), 'object', 'observation', 'activity'/'practice'. (I take the latter two to be interchangeable.)

Marx says that in traditional materialism 'objectivity (der Gegenstand) . . . is conceived only in the form of the *object* (*Objekt*) or of *observation* (*Anschauung*); not however as sensible *human activity, practice* . . . as activity *which belongs to the objective world* (*gegenständliche* Tätigkeit)'. To start with, what is the general sense of this distinction between 'objectivity' and 'object'? This is hardly a stock contrast and its meaning has largely to be distilled from the text. The latter suggests that 'objectivity' here denotes very generally that which 'stands against' (Gegenstand) us, the objective or 'external' world as such, 'reality', 'the sensible world': that about which we gain information by the use of our senses. Marx says that traditional materialism thinks this general notion in a specific form, namely, that of 'the object' or 'observation'. What is meant here by 'object' as distinct from 'objectivity' is elucidated firstly, by the pairing of 'object' with 'observation', and secondly, by the immediately following mention of what in the light of which traditional materialism is said to be deficient, viz. 'activity' or 'practice'. 'Anschauung' – here translated as 'observation' – means in the broadest sense simply a view (anschauem, to look at) about or at something. Its connected sense in classical German philosophy is that of a direct, immediate acquaintance with an object of thought which is apprehended in its individual reality.[11] The idea conveyed is that of an entirely passive awareness, a mirror-like 'view'.

What follows confirms and elucidates this. 'Object' conveys the idea of a world constituted and given in knowledge quite independently of any 'activity' or 'practice'[12] on the part of the 'subject',[13] an activity or practice which is 'sensible' (involving the sense-organs) and which 'belongs to the objective world' (is 'gegenständliche').

What Marx means by this latter characterization is at least two sorts of things. Firstly, he is drawing attention to the role of human practice in helping to constitute the character of the objective world in a straightforward material way. This is exemplified in the first instance by the way in which economic-productive activity changes the world: forests felled or grown, crops sown and harvested, new plants and animals cultivated, cities built, and so on.[14]

But his meaning is not limited to this. Remember that he is talking in very general terms about 'objectivity, reality, the sensible world'. He is also bidding us see, for example, social relations, characteristics of human beings, as being results of human practice. His point applies even further to knowledge of the world so constituted. He is rejecting views which ignore the role of practice in bringing about knowledge of the world, views which fail to see, for example, scientific 'facts' as being products of quite specific practices. This point looks forward to the views set out in most detail—though still fragmentarily—in the introduction to the *Grundrisse* written twenty years later.[15]

Secondly, Marx is indicating a materialist conception of practice as something to be analysed in terms of actual effects in the objective world in contrast to all subjectivist conceptions.

In this connection Marx notes more or less parenthetically (in the second sentence) that the recognition of the centrality of activity or practice is the strength of (German) idealism, even though, because it is an idealism, the activity is only abstract, is divorced from its real, sensible foundation, and its actual effects in the objective world.[16] Thus, if you like, traditional materialism is a philosophy of the abstract object (the real, sensible object considered in abstraction from transforming human practice) whilst (German) idealism is a philosophy of the abstract subject (human practice considered in abstraction from the real, sensible object).

But note also how Marx is expressing a new idea in old terminology: that of the 'subject'. This runs the risk of all manner of subjectivist misinterpretations of Marx's meaning. What he is in fact pointing towards is human productive activity of various sorts, different types of transformation of pre-existing materials. But this not only does not require, it positively excludes, a theorization in terms of the traditional notion of the 'subject' in any of its many forms. Thus economic productive practice is to be analysed and explained in terms of the ways in which labour-power is related to a set of objectively structured raw materials and instruments of labour, the way such power puts these into connection in accordance with the objective laws of the processes in question. The 'subject'-hood of the labour-power is not to the point, and in any case the labour-power is not the determinant factor in the situation.[17] Similar remarks apply to other types of practice.

In the final two sentences Marx draws some conclusions from the early part of the passage. In the first of these sentences – which relates more to Feuerbach than to traditional materialism as a whole – Marx says that Feuerbach's failure to understand the role of human practice in the constitution of the objective world has two related consequences, each of which is indeed the converse of the other. On the one hand, practice, practical activity, is conceived very narrowly and rigidly[18] by being restricted to a strictly utilitarian form typified by commercial dealing. (According to Feuerbach in *The Essence of Christianity* the Judaic religious conception rests on seeing things in terms of crude utility. And, he says, 'the practical view of things (Anschauung) is the grubby (schmutzige) view, stained (befleckte) by egoism'.[19] On the other hand, corresponding to this devaluation of human practice, theory is raised to the level of being what pertains to the distinctively human.

In the concluding sentence Marx says that as a consequence of this defect in Feuerbach's doctrines he 'does not grasp the meaning of "revolutionary", of "practical-critical" activity'. The import of this should be clearer when later theses (especially Thesis 4) have been elucidated. (This refers especially to the unfamiliar term '"practical-critical" activity'.) But for the moment it will suffice to say that Marx's meaning is that because Feuerbach does not grasp how practice goes to constitute the objective world as it exists, he does not grasp how practice may transform, revolutionize it either.

Thesis 2

> The question whether truth about the objective world is attained by human thinking – is not a question of theory, but a *practical* question. In practice must man prove the truth, that is reality and power, this-worldliness of his thinking. The dispute over the reality or non-reality of thinking – that is isolated from practice – is a purely *scholastic* question.[20]

Thesis 1 was about the role of practice in the constitution

of objectivity and in the constitution of knowledge of it. Thesis 2 is about the role of practice in the assessment of claims to knowledge about the objective world.[21]

Note that Marx is not saying, with empiricists and positivists in general, that truth-claims are to be assessed in terms of for example 'experience'. He is saying that they are to be assessed in terms of *practice*, that is, an activity of transformation. Again, he is not putting forward a pragmatist variant of empiricism/positivism: he is not saying that truth-claims are to be assessed in terms of 'usefulness' in general. He is saying that they are to be assessed in terms of the 'reality and power' of the claims.[22] What is the 'power' that is spoken of here? Clearly it is the power conferred by certain items of putative knowledge, and not by others, to serve as a basis for a capacity to transform the world in accordance with certain aims. The best commentary on Marx at this point is a few sentences from Engels' much later work on Feuerbach (in which Marx's *Theses* was first published).

> ... in what relation do our thoughts about the world surrounding us stand to this world itself? Is our thinking capable of knowledge of the real world? ... there [are] ... those who question the possibility of any knowledge, or at least of an exhaustive knowledge, of the world. ... The most telling refutation of this as of all other philosophical crotchets [Schrullen] is practice, namely, experiment and industry. If we are able to prove the correctness of our conception of a natural process by making it ourselves, bringing it into being out of its conditions and making it serve our own purposes into the bargain, then there is an end to the Kantian ungraspable 'thing-in-itself'.[23]

Thesis 3

> The materialist doctrine about change of circumstances and education forgets that circumstances are changed by men and the educator himself must be educated. Hence it must sunder society into two parts – of which one is superior to society.
> The coincidence of the changing of circumstances and of human activity or self-change can be conceived and rationally understood only as *revolutionary practice*.[24]

The first two theses criticized traditional materialism (in particular Feuerbach's) from a very general point of view. Thesis 3 turns to a critique of traditional materialist theory of

society. The first paragraph sets out an inadequacy in this
theory, and the second suggests an alternative view.

First the inadequacy registered in the initial paragraph.
Marx is here alluding to the following sort of view (held
especially by French Enlightenment materialists and by
Utopian socialists, French and English). On the one hand, the
environment, natural and social (in particular 'education')[25]
forms the people who live in it: people are formed by
'circumstances'. On the other hand, therefore, a change in
people requires a change in these 'circumstances', and in
particular a change in their 'education'.[26] Now, Marx says,
this ignores the fact that circumstances and education do not
change themselves: they are changed by people. But this
poses a problem for the doctrines in question. For, if people at
a certain time are formed by the prevailing circumstances and
education, whence could possibly come the tendency for
them to change those circumstances and education? In short,
whence could possibly come the new education of the edu-
cators of the rest of the people? The stock way out of this
closed circle was to assume (at least in effect) that some people
in society are exempt from the total conditioning by circumstances and these are the ones whose mission it is to change
the latter in such a way as to change people. In this sense
they form a part of society superior to the rest of society.

One can see this problem in the social theory of traditional
materialism as being of a piece with the position criticized
in Thesis 1. There the central point was the significance for
'objectivity, reality, the sensible world' and for knowledge,
of an assumed strict separation between 'object' and 'subject',
in particular ignoring the relations between the two instituted
by practice. Here there is added the idea of the asymmetric,
one-way determination of the 'subject' by the 'object'.
In Thesis 1, Marx had, through the concept of practice,
asserted the role of the latter (and, through it, of the role of
the 'subject') in constituting the 'object' (hence overcoming
traditional materialism's rigid separation between the two).
In this third thesis he is affirming, conversely, the role of
practice (looked at from the side of the 'object') in changing
the 'subject'. Better still, he is affirming that in practice there
is a simultaneous transformation of both its terms.

This absolutely central part of Marx's thinking[27] cannot be properly explicated until we come to Thesis 6. For the moment let us look at some parts of the slightly earlier *1844 Manuscripts*[28] which illustrate the point which Marx is making here even if they were not written in the context of this point.

'What', Marx asks at one point in the manuscripts, 'what . . . constitutes the alienation of labour?' He replies:

> First, the fact that labour is *external* to the worker, that is it does not belong to his intrinsic nature. . . . The worker therefore only feels himself outside his work, and in his work, feels outside himself. He feels at home when he is not working, and when he is working he does not feel at home. . . . As a result, therefore, man (the worker) only feels himself freely active in his animal functions – eating, drinking, procreating, . . . and in his human functions he no longer feels himself to be anything but an animal. What is animal becomes human and what is human becomes animal. Certainly eating, drinking, procreating etc., are also genuinely human functions. But taken abstractly, separated from the sphere of all other human activity and turned into sole and ultimate ends, they are animal functions.

Marx's answer here is in the subjectively shaded terms inseparable from the theoretical framework of 'alienation'. But this underlying point comes through: a certain type of practice (economic-productive practice involving wage-labour) brings about a characteristic fragmentation of the totality of distinctively human practices. Much later in the manuscripts occurs a passage which links up with what has just been found and forms an illustrative commentary on the third thesis. Marx writes here:

> When communist *artisans* associate with one another, theory, propaganda, etc., is their first end. But at the same time, as a result of this association, they acquire a new need – the need for society – and what appears as a means becomes an end. In this practical process the most splendid results are to be observed whenever French socialist workers are seen together. Such things as smoking, drinking, eating, etc., are no longer means of contact or means that bring them together. Associations, society and conversation, which again has association as its end, are enough for them; the brotherhood of man is no mere phrase with them, but a fact of life . . .

Thus a practical activity which was initiated by the need to transform their objective conditions is accompanied at the same time by a transformation of their personal practices, by a trend in the direction of overcoming their 'alienation'.

This was a central and continuing theme in Marx's thought. One aspect of it may be brought out here because of its political importance, namely, the idea that the revolutionary struggle of the oppressed is not related in a merely 'external' or instrumental way to the end of their liberation but is an absolutely essential part of the process of their liberation, so that genuine liberation excludes all forms of revolution 'from above': 'substitutionism', 'putschism', etc., and such exclusion is not an abstract moral demand but a political necessity.[29] The idea goes through Marx's work from beginning to end. Thus in *The German Ideology* it is said that:

> communism is for us not a state of affairs which is to be established, an ideal to which reality (will) have to adjust itself. We call communism the real movement which abolishes the present state of things. ... Both for the production on a mass scale of this communist consciousness, and for the success of the cause itself, the alteration of men on a mass scale is necessary, an alteration which can only take place in a practical movement, a *revolution*; this revolution is necessary, therefore, not only because the *ruling* class cannot be overthrown in any other way, but also because this class *overthrowing* it can only in a revolution succeed in ridding itself of all the muck of ages and become fitted to found society anew.[30]

Five years later Marx, addressing the Central Committee of the Committee of the Communist League, and opposing what he considered to be premature attempts at a reawakening of the revolutionary projects of 1848–49, said: 'We tell the workers: If you want to change conditions and make yourselves capable of government, you will have to undergo fifteen, twenty or fifty years of civil war.'[31] Again, over fifteen years later, in the programme of the First International, he enunciated the principle that 'the emancipation of the working classes must be conquered by the working classes themselves'.[32] Finally, in Marx's work on the civil war in France in 1870, a quarter of a century after the passage from *The German Ideology* cited above: 'The working class ... have no ready-made utopias to introduce *par decret du peuple*. They know that in order to work out their own emancipation ... they will have to pass through long struggles, through a series of historical processes, transforming circumstances and men.'[33] The last words seem almost to echo the third Thesis on Feuerbach still unpublished in Marx's notebooks.

Thesis 4

> Feuerbach starts from the fact of religious self-estrangement, of the duplication of the world into a religious and a secular one. His work consists in resolving the religious world into its secular basis. But that the secular basis takes off from itself and establishes itself as an independent realm in the clouds can only be explained in terms of the inwardly riven and inwardly contradictory character of this secular basis. Therefore this itself must both be understood in its contradiction and revolutionized in practice. Thus once for example the earthly family is revealed as the secret of the holy family, the former must itself be destroyed in theory and in practice.[34]

Theses 1 and 2 set out a very general critique of traditional materialism, Thesis 3 particularized this critique with respect to the theory of society. Thesis 4 criticizes Feuerbach's account of religion specifically, though this critique has a quite general significance which will be made explicit in subsequent theses.

The thesis falls into three parts: the first two sentences, the third, and the last two.

In the first two sentences Marx summarizes, in allusive fashion, Feuerbach's theory of religion. This is (only a little less briefly) as follows.[35] Individual human beings have only limited power, love, knowledge. But humanity as a species has these qualities in potentially unlimited measure. Religion is a matter of the projection of the latter which, as actually pertaining to the species, lie outside of any human individual, onto an imaginary bearer who is other than every human individual – and this men call God.

In the next, third sentence, Marx both criticizes Feuerbach (the emphasis being methodological rather than substantive) and indicates an alternative view. The criticism is, briefly, this. Feuerbach really does little more than register a 'fact' (the fact of religious self-estrangement[36]) about what is the case. (Or, putting it by anticipation in the light of the eleventh thesis, he merely 'interprets' a situation.) Human beings live under the sign of the estrangement of their species-being (God). The real human family gives rise to the imaginary divine family. Feuerbach does not even pose the question – far less answer it – as to why this process of estrangement occurs, he does not explain it.

From what has been said so far the form of Marx's answer, his view of religion alternative to Feuerbach's is clear, programmatically at least. This situation of estrangement must be seen as the result of a specific social situation: the religious world which Feuerbach has 'resolved' into its secular basis is a product of 'the inwardly riven and inwardly contradictory character of this secular basis'.[37] Marx is already working from the standpoint that 'social being determine consciousness'.[38]

(It is unnecessary, for the purposes of this brief commentary, to go into the details of Marx's theory of religion in the writings immediately preceding the 'Theses'. It was briefly this.[39] In a capitalist society, as in any society, people are united by the common essence of their species. But in a capitalist society, based on mutual competition and antagonism, what is immediately experienced is not this common essence, what unites people, but rather what separates them.[40] So the qualities of the common essence are experienced as real but as pertaining to something other than humanity. In other words they are projected onto a transcendental being, God. It is not difficult to see here both the similarities and the differences between such a view and Feuerbach's.)

Now in the final two sentences of the thesis Marx draws some consequences from the position just sketched. If religion is a product of a definite form of society, of definite practices, then the elimination of religion cannot be achieved just by a theoretical critique, even though this is undoubtedly necessary: the secular basis which generates and sustains religion must certainly be 'understood in its contradiction' and the earthly family, the secular basis of the holy family, must be 'destroyed in theory'. But beyond that it is necessary to change this secular basis itself: it must be 'revolutionized', 'destroyed' in practice. This then is the meaning of '"practical-critical" activity' at the end of Thesis 1: corresponding to criticism of a *theoretical* kind, the aim of which is the understanding of a situation, there is 'criticism' of a *practical* kind which materially transforms a situation. As Marx wrote in a slightly earlier article: 'The weapon of criticism cannot . . . replace criticism by weapons.'[41]

Thus in this Thesis we see the essentially political effects induced by epistemological deficiencies: traditional materialism can give no adequate basis for a struggle against for example religion.

It is clear that a criticism similar to that which Marx brings against Feuerbach's intellectualist approach to religion can be made of more recent approaches to situations like racism, sexism, consumerism.[42] This is that they are not understood in terms of their social genesis and real functioning, so that the fight against them to that extent is confined to a 'superstructural' level.

Thesis 5

> Feuerbach, not satisfied with *abstract thinking*, appeals to *observation*; but he does not conceive the sensible world as *practical* human activity involving the senses.[43]

What is said here is substantially only a reprise of part of what has already been said in Thesis 1, and one may therefore pass on immediately to the next thesis, which resumes the critique of Feuerbach on religion initiated in Thesis 4.

Thesis 6

> Feuerbach resolves the essence of religion into the essence of *man*. But the essence of man is no abstraction indwelling in each separate individual. In its reality it is the ensemble of social relations.
>
> Feuerbach, who does not enter into the critique of this real essence, is hence obliged:
>
> (1) to abstract from the course of history and to set off the religious attitude as something self-contained, and to assume an abstract – *isolated* – human individual.

(2) Hence the essence can be conceived only as 'genus', as an inner, mute, universal character uniting the many individuals in a *natural* way.[44]

The content of the first sentence is familar: it is only a different way of putting what is said at the beginning of Thesis 4. The following two sentences state a view on the subject of the human 'essence', first negatively and then positively. Negatively, Marx rejects all essentialist theories, that is, all theories about human beings, society, history, which begin from characterizations of the intrinsic natures of individuals, whether such natures are conceived of in transcendental (for example Christian) or in naturalistic (for example Hobbesian) terms: whether conceived of as historically fixed or conceived of as subject to change, the question concerns the fixing on the individual as the theoretically primary element.[45]

This comes out even more clearly in the following sentence in which Marx puts the point positively: 'in its reality (the essence of man) is the ensemble of social relations'. Once again Marx puts a new theoretical point (the point of departure for the study of human beings is their social relations) in 'old-speak' terminology, talk of 'essences'. (See the remark in the commentary on Thesis 1 on Marx's use of 'subject'.) Doing so, moreover, strains the latter to the point of incoherence. For in the traditional discourse which gives the term a meaning, 'essences' pertain of necessity to individuals as contrasted with relations, whereas he here characterizes 'essences' precisely in terms of relations. In such a conception, which was to be given clear development and made the basis of his later work,[46] individuals are to be regarded not as the origin or constituting basis of their relations but rather as the 'bearers' of those relations.[47]

At this point I want to return for a moment to a thread dropped in the remarks on Thesis 3. One can now see more clearly the viewpoint from which Marx criticized the traditional materialist social theory and the nature of that criticism. This traditional theory sharply separated individuals and their social relations, which were conceived of as being purely 'external' to them. The further development of the theory consisted in an oscillation between these elements:

the individuals on the one hand, and their relations on the
other. To start with the relations – 'circumstances and education' – are assigned the primary determining role. But in
the light of the problem as to how these relations can change,
the emphasis shifts and individuals – some of them anyway –
are assigned a determining role. But these are simply variations within an invariant framework. For Marx, however,
what is primary are relations which confer on the individuals
which are their terms definite characteristics, motives for
action and so on. Furthermore, these relational structures
have inbuilt tendencies to change – basically, 'contradictions' – which express themselves, work themselves out,
through the people who stand in the relations, and in particular through their actions. Thus on the one hand, 'circumstances and education' – social relations – are shaped by people,
but, on the other hand, by virtue of the consequent new
relations, the people themselves are different. This is 'the
coincidence of the changing of circumstances and of human
activity of self-change'.

At the beginning of the second paragraph Marx comments
that Feuerbach 'does not enter into the critique of this real
essence'. The term 'critique' is worth a comment here for it
is one which runs right through Marx's work. Thus two
years before the composition of the 'Theses' Marx had
written a *Critique of Hegel's Philosophy of Right*, his first
major published work in political economy was called a
contribution to the 'critique' thereof, and the sub-title of
Capital is: *Critique of Political Economy*. The term meant,
for Marx, not just 'criticism' in the ordinary sense, not just
the demonstration of error, but also an exhibition of the
origin and genesis of the errors. He explains the matter in the
critique of Hegel just referred to. Here he characterizes
'vulgar' or 'dogmatic' critique as criticism within the framework of what is being criticized, as when 'formerly the
dogma of the Holy Trinity . . . was demolished by the
contradiction of one and three'. This contrasts with 'true
criticism (Kritik)' which 'shows the inner genesis of the Holy
Trinity in the human brain. It describes the act of its birth.
So the truly philosophical criticism of the present state
constitution not only shows up contradictions as existing, it

explains them, it comprehends their genesis, their necessity'.[48] Thus it was for a failure to give a 'critique' in this sense that Marx criticized Feuerbach in Thesis 3 and it was the programme for such a critique that Marx gave in the same Thesis.

To resume, Marx goes on to say that inasmuch as Feuerbach does not give a critique in this sense, that is does not locate the genesis and conditions for functioning of religion in certain social relations, he necessarily abstracts the phenomenon of religion from society and history and treats it as something self-subsistent. And for the same reason this self-subsistent 'attitude' is located in what remains when social relations are ignored, namely, (hypothetically) isolated individuals who are 'abstract' in the sense of being abstracted from the social relations which in fact confer on them their specificities. Furthermore (and this is Marx's second point) since Feuerbach abstracts from the real *social* character of what makes human beings members of a commonality – their standing in certain sorts of relations to nature and to one another (especially *productive* relations) – what unites the multiplicity of individuals can only be conceived as some purely natural characteristic which they share as physical, biological entities.

Thesis 7

> Hence Feuerbach does not see that the 'religious attitude' itself is a social product and that the abstract individual which he analyzes belongs to a definite form of society.[49]

The first clause of this thesis only sums up what has just gone before. The second clause makes explicit an implication of the doctrines just outlined and in effect poses a question (precisely *what* form of society?) which is in fact answered in Theses 9 and 10. But before this answer is presented Marx generalizes the insight illustrated in the preceding criticism of Feuerbach's traditional materialist view of religion.

Thesis 8

> All social life is essentially *practical*. All mysteries that turn theory

towards mysticism find their rational solution in human practice
and in the comprehension of this practice.[50]

The first sentence puts more sharply than ever the standpoint of the *Theses* so far. 'All social life is essentially *practical*'
means: social life is a complex of (material) *practices*, of
activities of transformation of pre-existing states of affairs
into others. This is to deny, amongst other things, that social
life is to be looked at as primarily contemplative-intellectual,
as based on personal relations, affective or otherwise, and so
on.

Therefore (and this is the content of the second sentence)
if there is something about social life which is difficult to
understand, mysterious, and which, on that account, is
liable to occasion mystical, obscurantist doctrines, then the
methodologically correct path to its adequate understanding
is an examination of the relevant area of the practices which
constitute that society ('rational solution' as in the solution
of a puzzle) and the correct path to an overcoming of the
material basis of a tendency towards mysticism is a change in
that practice ('rational solution' in the sense of 'resolution':
'practical criticism'). This is the view which is already
implicit (if highly so) in Thesis 1, and which has been
exemplified in the particular case of religion in the last few
theses. (Marx much later exemplified it in the case of another
'religion' – what he called 'this religion of everyday life', the
world of 'vulgar' political economy.[51])

This general point completes (with Thesis 7) the pre-
paration of the ground for the next two theses. Religion is a
'mystery' and is bound up with the mysticism of the 'abstract
individual'. What is the social practice which corresponds to
such an idea? What is the 'definite form of society' to which
such an individual belongs? Answers to these questions are
asserted in the following theses.

Thesis 9

The highest point attained by materialism based on observation,
that is materialism which does not comprehend the sensible world as
practical activity, is the observation of separate individuals and of
civil society.[52]

Thesis 10

> The standpoint of the old materialism is civil society, the standpoint
> of the new, human society or social humanity.[53]

Theses 9 and 10 may be taken together as specifying at once
the social basis of the traditional materialism which has been
criticized throughout the 'Theses' and also 'the new materialism' from the point of view of which this criticism has been
conducted. With this I return to Thesis 1 in which both
themes were introduced.

To begin with, traditional 'materialism based on observation' (der anschauende Materialismus) is said to be the
point of view (Anschauung)[54] of separate individuals in
'civil society' (bürgerliche Gesellschaft).[55] What does this
mean?

First, 'civil society'. This was a term introduced by English
writers in the eighteenth century and taken over by
French authors, and by Hegel among others. It acquired its
meaning in the context of a theory which distinguished a
domain where people pursued private, particular, individual
ends from a domain concerned with public, universal,
common ones. The first – the sphere of economic behaviour,
the family, and so on – was 'civil society'; the second was the
sphere of the political, the State. For the materialist writers on
society already referred to, civil society was in a definite sense
the primary domain: individuals pursuing ends set for them
by their particularities as individuals, the State having the
job of regulating these individual actions so as to allow a
maximally smooth functioning of the whole.

Now for Marx these allegedly primary individuals are
'abstract' because they are considered in abstraction from the
underlying network of social relations which confer on them
their characteristics, tendencies to action, and so on. A
given individual in civil society – for example a private
producer – is immediately aware of himself or herself as
someone acting from original characteristics and tendencies
independently of other individuals similarly endowed. The
reality is that the social relations of all these individuals,
'invisible' at the level of everyday experiences, confer these

characteristics and tendencies on them (considered as centres of economic behaviour for example). In other words, from the point of view of awareness of self, the individual of civil society relates immediately to the natural and social world (s/he is a Robinson Crusoe in a world of Robinson Crusoes[56]) whereas in reality s/he does so only through the mediation of a complex of social practices. Similar remarks apply to the individual knowing subject of the traditional materialism which in its assumed direct confrontation with the objective world is the Crusoe of political economy transposed to the domain of epistemology.[57] And the 'new materialism' is precisely a materialism conceived from the standpoint of the primacy of social relations, social practices: 'human society or social humanity'.[58]

Thesis 11

> The philosophers have only *interpreted* the world in different ways, the point is to *change* it.[59]

It should be apparent by now that the famous eleventh thesis in all its lapidary brevity, its enigmatic simplicity, is far from that crude pragmatism in terms of which it has been frequently understood. It in fact brings to a fine point, distills to a quintessence, the whole content of the preceding theses.

Two major threads have gone through the 'Theses' so far. On the one hand there is the essentially 'passivistic' character of traditional materialism, its failure to recognize the role of human activity in constituting both objectivity and that activity itself (both 'object' and 'subject'). On the other hand, there is the characterization of Marx's materialism and the central role in it of precisely that transformative activity or *practice*.

The last of the 'Theses' is constructed on just this contrast: on the one hand, 'the philosophers', especially traditional materialist philosophers,[60] and their *interpretation* of the world, on the other, by implication, the new materialism and its emphasis on *changing* the world.

'The philosophers have only *interpreted* the world in different ways . . . .' The meaning of this has already been

indicated in the remarks above on Thesis 4. 'To interpret':
to spell out the meaning or significance of something –
paradigmatically, to give the sense of a text, which is something 'given', a 'datum', not there to be changed but to yield
up its meaning. This is the point of Marx's critique of
Feuerbach's theory of religion: that it merely describes,
limns, lays bare the character of a state of affairs as it is without
explaining it, without making clear the conditions of its
possibility.[61] (As for the idealists: Hegel's philosophical Owl
of Minerva flies only at dusk after the works of the day are
finished.[62])

'. . . the point is to *change* it.' The point is to change the
world because, to start with, truth-claims about the world can
only be evaluated as a result of changing the world in a
practice. Then again, since views about the world, attitudes,
propensities for action (for example the entire 'religious
attitude'), are rooted in definite social practices, such views,
attitudes and propensities can, in the final analysis, only be
changed by changing these practices, that is by changing a
part of the world. In other words, since both error and what
'the philosophers' have held to be desirable situations have
material roots, it is insufficient, even from the point of view of
'the philosophers' themselves, to try to eliminate error and
institute the desirable whilst staying within the confines of
merely theoretical criticism.[63]

The meaning of the eleventh thesis can also be brought out
in another way. In the manuscript of *The German Ideology*
Marx has the following marginal note: 'So-called *objective*
historiography consisted . . . in treating historical relations
separately from activity. Reactionary character.'[64] Of
'objective historiography' we can say that it is an instance of
historians having only interpreted the world . . . Such
historiography confines itself to describing the 'surface'
results of human practices without going into the specific
character of those practices which are the springs, the
mechanisms of production of those results. Thus this is a
point similar to that which Marx makes throughout the
'Theses' about traditional materialism. Why does Marx say
that such historiography is 'reactionary'? For one thing
because to the extent that only overall results and not specific

mechanisms are investigated, the course of history assumes the appearance of automatism, of independence from intervention, something which favours the continuance of what is rather than what might be. More specifically, insofar as it does not reveal the moving springs of historical change it does not yield the information which a revolutionary needs to intervene rationally in order to influence the direction and pace of change. Marx's analyses in his later work were 'non-objective' in the sense that the key *analytical* concepts (above all, that of class-struggle) were ones which provided an Archimedian point for active intervention in the course of history, for changing the world.[65] And it is in this sense that *genuinely* objective historiography (indeed social theory in general) – which investigates the structural-causal springs of social change – is 'partisan' in giving relevant and indispensable theoretical weapons to those in whose interests it is to change the world.[66] The 'Theses' thus provide a quite distinctive way of regarding the 'fact-value problem'. But that is another story.

> It is impossible for an expositor not to write too little for some, and too much for others. He can only judge what is necessary by his own experience; and how long soever he may deliberate, will at last explain many lines which the learned will think impossible to be mistaken, and omit many for which the ignorant will want this help. These are censures merely relative, and must be quietly endured.
>
> Dr Johnson[67]

Notes

References to Marx's original texts are to the Marx-Engels *Werke* (Berlin 1956), abbreviated as MEW: References to English translations are, where possible, to Marx–Engels, *Collected Works* (London 1975), abbreviated as MECW. If the work has not yet appeared in this edition, reference is made, if possible, to Marx–Engels, *Selected Works in Three Volumes* (Moscow 1970), or, if not available there, to other editions specified at the point of reference. In the following quotations from German, the German letter *eszet* (*sz*) is represented by the English B.

1 *For Marx* (London 1969), p. 36.
2 Marx's text appeared first in the separate book edition (1888) of Engels's *Ludwig Feuerbach and the End of Classical German Philosophy* (first published 1886 in *Neue Zeit*), as 'Marx on Feuerbach', under the heading '1. ad Feuerbach'. The title *Theses on Feuerbach* stems from the 1932 edition by the Institute of Marxism-Leninism (Moscow) of Marx's original text, with reference to Engel's description in the 'Foreword' to the 1888 edition of *Ludwig Feuerbach* (MESW, III, p. 336). The present translation is of Marx's original text as it appears in MEW, III, pp. 5–7.
3 Engels, *loc. cit.* note 2.
4 The passages in the earlier works of Marx and Engels relevant to Feuerbach are cited in Alfred Schmidt, *Emanzipatorische Sinnlichkeit. Ludwig Feuerbach's antropologischer Materialismus* (Müchen 1973), especiality pp. 17ff. See also W. Schuffenhauer, *Feuerbach und der Junge Marx* (Berlin 1965).
5 Other commentaries in English on the *Theses* as a whole will be found in Hook and Rotenstreich (*op. cit.*, note 6 below) and in E. Bloch, *On Karl Marx* (New York 1971). See also L. Goldmann, 'L'idéologie allemande et les Théses sur Feuerbach', reprinted in his *Marxisme et sciences humaines* (Paris 1970), especially pp. 170ff. There is a commentary on some of the *Theses* in A. S. Vazquez, *The Philosophy of Praxis* (London 1977), pp. 115ff.
6 These are, in alphabetical order of translator: Anon in MESW, I, pp. 13–15 (variants of this version appear in various anthologies). Anon, MECW, V, pp. 3–5. T. B. Bottomore in Marx, *Selected Writing in Sociology and Social Philosophy*, T. B. Bottomore and M. Rubel (eds.) (Harmondsworth 1963), pp. 82–4. L. D. Easton and K. E. Guddat in *Writings of the Young Marx on Philosophy and Society*, Easton and Guddat (tr., and ed.) (New York 1967), pp. 400–402. S. Hook, *From Hegel to Marx*, rev. ed. (Ann Arbor 1962), ch. 8. R. Pascal in Marx–Engels, *The German Ideology*,

ps 1 and 3, plus *Theses on Feuerbach* (Calcutta 1945), pp. 189–91. N. Rotenstreich, *Basic Problems of Marx's Philosophy* (Indianapolis 1965), ch. 2. I have also seen a roneoed translation by Rip Bulkeley (dated January 1978).

7　I am indebted to the following for reading earlier versions of the translation and making comments: Dr Jan Bruch, Mr Rip Bulkeley, Dr Z. Hanfi, Prof. J. O'Malley, Dr D. McLellan, Dr M. Hudson, Dr M. Roth. I have not always taken their advice and the responsibility for the translation as it stands is mine alone. Dr John Burnheim made some very helpful remarks on the commentary.

8　Der Hauptmangel alles bisherigen Materialismus (den Feuerbachs-chen mit eingerechnet) ist, daB der Gegenstand, die Wirklichkeit, die Sinnlichkeit nur unter der Form des *Objekts order der Anschauung* gefaBt wird; nicht aber als *sinnlich menschliche Tätigkeit, Parxis*, nicht subjektiv. Daher die *tätgie* Seite abstrakt im Gegensatz zu dem Materialismus von dem Idealismus – der näturlich die wirkliche, sinnliche Tätigkeit als solche nicht kennt – entwickelt. Feuerbach will sinnliche – von den Gedankenobjekten wirklich unterschiedne Objekte – aber er faBt die menschliche Tätigkeit selbst nicht als *gegenständliche* Tätigkeit. Er betrachtet daher im 'Wesen des Christen-thums' nur das theoretische Verhalten als das echt menschliche, während die Praxis nur in ihrer schmutzig jüdischen Erscheinungs-form gefaBt und fixiert wird. Er begreift daher nicht die Bedeutung der 'revolutionären', der 'praktisch-kritischen' Tätigkeit.

9　For other discussions of traditional materialism see Marx's contribu-tion on the subject to Marx–Engels, *The Holy Family*, ch. 6, 3, d.

10　'Sinnlich' 'Sinnlichkeit': 'Sensuous' in its older meaning (see *Shorter OED*, 3rd ed., II, p. 1842) is an accurate rendering of 'sinnlich' (and hence 'sensuousness' for 'Sinnlichkeit') and has been used by many translators. But it now has other overtones which make it unsuitable for bringing over Marx's meaning. With considerable hesitation I have chosen 'sensible', though this is somewhat 'technical'.

11　See for example Kant, *Critique of Pure Reason*, A320/B377 (Kemp-Smith's translation): 'Knowledge . . . is either *intuition* [Anschauung] or *concept* . . . The former relates immediately to the object and is single, the latter refers to it mediately by means of a feature which several things may have in common.' See for example A. Lalande, *Vocabulaire technique et critique de la philosophie*, 10th ed. (Paris 1968), pp. 537ff, for a survey of other references and meanings in the litera-ture. 'Anschauung' is (or should be) a nightmare for the English translator. The more or less standard translation is 'intuition'. (See for example the above passage from Kant.) But this has undesirable overtones from ordinary usage. 'Idea' or 'sense-impression' in Locke-Berkeley-Hume tradition is close, but has unwanted subjecti-vist reverberations. 'Perception', 'observation', 'contemplation' – none of the renderings which occur in current versions captures the original. I have finally adopted 'observation' because it seems better than any of the others to capture the 'passiveness' of 'Anschauung', and because it permits some approximation to the pun in Thesis 9.

12   'Praxis' is more 'natural' in German than 'praxis' in English, despite the increasing use of the term. Therefore I have chosen to render it by an ordinary, fairly non-technical term in English, though of course it has a special place in Marx's thought, particularly in his earlier writings.

13   Is there an echo of Hegel in Marx's contrast between 'Gegenstand' and 'Objekt'? (See for example Hegel's *Encyclopedia*, pt. I (the 'Lesser Logic'), sec. 193: 'By 'object' [Objekt] is commonly understood ... something which is concrete and *completely* independent in itself. ... That the object [Objekt] is also an object to us [Gegenstand] and is external to something else, will be more precisely seen, when it puts itself in *contrast* with the *subjective*.' W. Wallace's translation (revised, W. S.), *The Logic of Hegel* 2nd ed. (Oxford 1902), p. 329. The contrast poses considerable difficulties for the English translator, since both terms would, in a philosophical context at least, normally be rendered by the same English word, viz. 'object'. The implicit contrast of 'Objekt' and 'Subjekt' more or less preempts 'object' for 'Objekt'. The rendering of 'Gegenstand' by 'objectivity' has shortcomings. For example, this has a different and specific German equivalent ('Objektivität'); it has other meanings in English unwanted here; and there is a verbal similarity with 'object' not present in the original. But I have not been able to think of a better way out. As regards 'gegenständlich', its translation by 'objective' has the unfortunate consequence (given the above renderings) of perhaps appearing to refer back to 'object' rather than to 'objectivity'. The only alternative to 'objective' here seems to be the very slight paraphrase adopted in my rendering.

14   See the relevant passages in *The German Ideology*, MECW, V: pp. 38ff, 58.

15   *Grundrisse*, Introduction, sec. 3 (Harmondsworth 1973), pp. 100ff. On the idea of knowledge as the result of a process of production see L. Althusser, *For Marx* (London 1969), pp. 182ff, etc., L. Althusser and E. Balibar, *Reading Capital* (London 1970), index, sv, 'practice, theoretical'. Also J. Ravetz, *Scientific Knowledge and Its Social Problems* (Oxford 1971), pt. 2.

16   For criticism of Hegel's idea of practice as idealist see Marx's *1844 Manuscripts*, MECW, III, pp. 329ff. Also *Grundrisse, loc. cit.*, previous note.

17   See *Capital*, I, (Harmondsworth 1976), especially p. 286.

18   'Fixiert'. This probably has the sense both of 'demarcated' (as in fixing the meaning of a word) and also of 'made rigid' (hypostasizing of one aspect of practice).

19   Cited from the 1841 edition of *Das Wesen des Christentums* by Ernst Bloch in *Das Prinzip Hoffnung*, I (Berlin 1953), p. 284. On the whole question see ch. 11 of Feuerbach's book. The 'grubby' is meant to allude, inter al., to 'money grubbing'. See also Marx, 'On the Jewish Question', MECW, III.

20 Die Frage, ob dem menschlichen Denken gegenständliche Wahrheit
    zukomme – ist keine Frage der Theorie, sondern eine *praktische*
    Frage. In der Praxis muß der Mensch die Wahrheit, i.e. Wirklichkeit
    und Macht, Diesseitigkeit seines Denkens beweisen. Der Streit
    über die Wirklichkeit oder Nichtwirklichkeit des Denkens – das von
    der Praxis isoliert ist – ist eine rein *scholastische* Frage.

21 ' . . . truth about the objective world . . . ': ' . . . gegenständliche
    Wahrheit . . . ' This is generally translated 'objective truth', but such
    a rendering does not seem to me to bring over the force of the adjective.
    'Objective' in 'objective truth' usually has (or at least tends to have)
    the force of 'free from subjective bias (etc.)' Marx is much more
    directly speaking of truth about what is objective to us, the 'Gegen-
    stand' of the beginning of Thesis 1.

22 ' . . . reality and power . . . ': ' . . . Wirklichkeit und Macht . . . ':
    Prof. John O'Malley (private communication) suggests using 'actua-
    lity' for 'reality' to bring out the linguistic connection with 'power'
    ('Wirklichkeit' being etymologically linked with 'wirken', 'to act
    upon/cause'). (This would also preserve the etymological parallel of
    'Wirklichkeit' and 'actuality'). Such a move is certainly necessary
    in translating Hegel, where there is an important distinction between
    'Wirklichkeit' and 'Realität'. But I am inclined to think that Marx
    is using it non-technically here and that 'reality' is more natural.

23 *Ludwig Feuerbach and the End of the Classical German Philosophy*,
    MESW, III, pp. 346, 347. There is a longer passage of similar import
    in Engel's introduction to the English edition of *Socialism: Utopian
    and Scientific*, MESW, III, 101f. See also Lenin's commentary on
    the Feuerbach passage just referred to in *Materialism and Empirio-
    Criticism, Collected Works*, XIV, pp. 101ff – also pp. 104f and 120.

24 Die materialistische Lehre von der Veränderung der Umstände und
    der Erziehung vergißt, daß die Umstände von den Menschen
    verändert und der Erzieher selbst erzogen werden muß. Sie muß
    daher die Gesellschaft in zwei Teile – von denen der eine über ihr
    erhaben ist – sondieren. Das Zusammenfallen das Andern[s] der
    Umstände und der menschlichen Tätigkeit oder Selbstveränderung
    knur els revolutionäre Praxis gefaßt und rationall verstanden werden.

25 'Education' in English is rather narrower in meaning than 'Erziehung',
    which includes what in English would be expressed by, say, 'upbring-
    ing'. But then there would be no way of bringing over the verbal
    continuity with 'Erzieher' ('educator') a little further on.

26 'The materialist doctrine about the change of circumstances and
    education . . . ': 'Die materialistische Lehre von der Veränderung
    der Umstände und der Erziehung . . . ' The German here is ambigu-
    ous as between 'the materialist doctrine about change of circumstances
    and (about) education' and 'the materialist doctrine about change of
    circumstances and (about the change of) education'. I have left the
    English correspondingly ambiguous. In any event nothing of syste-
    matic significance seems to hang on it.

27 See the assertion of this point in *Capital*, I. (Harmondsworth 1976), p. 283.

28 MECW, III, pp. 274f and 313. There are endless examples of this process of simultaneous change of 'subject' and 'object' in the literature of revolution, particularly in that of the liberation struggles in the 'underdeveloped' world. See for example Jack Belden, *China Shakes the World* (New York 1970), William Hinton, *Fanshen* (New York 1968), especially pt. 4, Che Guevara, *Venceremos* (London 1969), especially pp. 57ff, 182ff, Frantz Fanon, *A Dying Colonialism* (Harmondsworth 1970). In the last cited see especially the gripping account (pp. 33ff, 87ff, etc.) of the transformation of the patriarchal Algerian family, with regard to the liberation of women, under the force of the exigencies of war.

29 This is an important element in the thought of Paulo Freire. See for example his *Pedagogy of the Oppressed* (New York 1971). It is also a theme in the work of Gramsci, particularly the earlier work, in his recognition that class-consciousness could not be imported into the working-class in a purely 'educational' manner from outside but had to grow out of the workers' own struggles – in Gramsci's situation at least, in the struggles around the factory councils. See for example Gramsci, *Selections from Political Writings (1910–20)* (London 1977), especially pt. 2. Also the material in A. Davidson, *Antonio Gramsci. An Intellectual Biography* (London 1977), especially ch. 3.

30 MECW, V, pp. 49 and 52f.

31 Marx, *Political Writings*, I: *The Revolutions of 1848* (Harmondsworth 1973), p. 341.

32 MESW, II, p. 19. See H. Draper, 'The principle of self-emancipation in Marx and Engels' in R. Miliband and J. Saville (eds.), *The Socialist Register 1971* (London 1971).

33 MESW, II, p. 224.

34 Feuerbach geht von dem Faktum der religiösen Selbstentfremdung, der Verdopplung der Welt in eine religiöse und eine weltliche aus. Seine Arbeit besteht darin, die religiöse Welt in ihre weltliche Grundlage aufzulösen. Aber daß die weltliche Grundlage sich von sich selbst abhebt und sich ein selbständiges Reich in den Wolken fixiert, ist nur aus der Selbstzerrissenheit und Sichselbstwidersprechen dieser weltlichen Grundlage zu erklären. Diese selbst muß also in sich selbst sowohl in ihrem Widerspruch verstanden als praktisch revolutioniert werden. Also nachdem z.B. die irdische Familie als das Geheimnis der heiligen Familie entdeckt ist, muß nun erstere selbst theoretisch und praktisch vernichtet werden.

35 For a somewhat more detailed account of Feuerbach's theory of religion see for example Karl Löwith, *From Hegel to Nietzsche* (New York 1967), pp. 331ff.

36 The grounds for rendering 'Selbstentfremdung' as 'self-estrangement' rather than as 'self-alienation', as is more frequent, can be found rehearsed in Martin Milligan's 'Translator's note on terminology',

s.v. 'Entäussern' and 'Entfremden' in his version of Marx's *Economic and Philosophic Manuscripts of 1844* (Moscow n.d.), pp. 11f.

37 See the slightly earlier articles 'On the Jewish Question' and 'Contribution to the Critique of Hegel's Philosophy of Law. Introduction' both in MECW.

38 Preface to *A Contribution to the Critique of Political Economy*, MESW, I, p. 503.

39 See especially Marx's two articles cited in note 37 above. For a fuller account of Marx's early theory of religion see for example Löwith, *op. cit.*, note 35 above, pp. 347ff.

40 This is a persisting theme in Marx. See for example *Theories of Surplus-Value*, I (Moscow 1969), p. 409.

41 'Contribution to the Critique of Hegel's Philosophy of Law. Introduction' MECW, III, p. 182.

42 See for example the remarks on consumerism (a propos Illich) by S. Bowles and H. Gintis in their *Schooling in Capitalist America* (New York 1976), pp. 256ff. See also Richard Lichtman, 'Capitalism and consumption', *Socialist Revolution*, I (1970), 83–96.

43 Feuerbach, mit dem *abstrakten Denken* nicht zufrieden, will die *Anschauung*; aber er faBt die Sinnlichkeit nicht als *praktische* menschlich-sinnliche Tätigkeit.

44 Feuerbach löst das religiöse Wesen in das *menschliche* Wesen auf. Aber das menschliche Wesen ist kein dem einzelnen Individuum inwohnendes Abstraktum. In seiner Wirklichkeit ist es das ensemble der gesellschaftlic hen Verhältnisse.
    Feuerbach, der auf die Kritik dieses wirklichen Wesens nicht eingeht, ist daher gezwungen:
    (1) von dem geschichtlichen Verlauf zu abstrahieren und das religiöse Gemüt für sich zu fixieren, und ein abstrakt – *isoliert* – menschliches Individuum vorauszusetzen.
    (2) Das Wesen kann daher nur als 'Gattung', als innere, stumme, die vielen Individuen *natürlich* verbindende Allgemeinheit gefaBt werden.

45 A view classically expressed by one of the frequent objects of Marx's criticism, J. S. Mill: 'Human beings in society have no properties but those which are derived from, and may be resolved into, the laws of the nature of individual man'. *System of Logic*, bk. 6, ch. 7, sec. 1. This runs right through bourgeois social theory from its classical representatives like Max Weber to epigones like Karl Popper ('methodological individualism').

46 For example *Grundrisse*: 'Society does not consist of individuals, but expresses the sum of interrelations, the relations within which these individuals stand.' (Harmondsworth 1973), p. 265. Also Marx's 'Notes on Adolph Wagner' in *Texts on Method*, T. Carver (tr.) (Oxford 1975), p. 201. For a recent reemphasis on this see the excellent paper by Roy Bhaskar, 'On the possibility of social scientific knowledge and the limits of naturalism'. *J. Th. Social Behaviour*, VIII (1978), 1–28, and *Issues in Marxist Philosophy* Volume III.

47 See for example *Capital*, III (Moscow 1962) pp. 798, 857f. It was Althusser and Balibar who first drew attention to the 'Träger'-concept in *Capital*. See their *Reading Capital* (London 1970), index, sv 'support'. [More recently Althusser has become, at the very least, ambiguous about the generality of the concept, appearing at times to want to restrict it to capitalism. See his *Essays in Self-Criticism* (London 1976), pp. 202, 206].

48 MECW, III, p. 91. All this is not to say that Marx's notion of 'critique' was univocal in all respects throughout his work. See on this J. Rancière's contribution to the first edition of *Lire le Capital*, reedition (*Line 1 Capital*, III, Paris 1973) translated on 'The concept of 'critique' in 'Critique of Political Economy', *Theoretical Practice* nos. 1, 2. 6 (1972), and *Economy and Society*, V, p. 3 (1976).

49 Feuerbach sieht daher nicht, daB das 'religiöse Gemüt' selbst gesellschaliches Produkt ist und daB das abstrakte Individuum, das er analysiert, einer bestimmten Gesellschaftsform angehört.

50 Alles gesellschaftliche Leben ist wesentlich *praktisch*. Alle Mysterien, welche die Theorie zum Mystizism [us] veranlassen, finden ihre rationelle Lösung in der menschlichen Praxis und in dem Begreifen dieser Paraxis.

51 *Capital*, III (Moscow 1962), p. 809 (MEW, XXV, p. 838). In *Theories of Surplus Value*, III (Moscow 1971), p. 453, he calls the same thing 'a kind of fiction without fantasy, a religion of the vulgar'.

52 Das Höchste, wozu der anschauende Materialismus kommt, d.h. der Materialismus, der die Sinnlichkeit nicht als praktische Tätigkeit begreift, ist die Anschauunglder elnzelnen Individuen und der bürgerlichen Gesellschaft.

53 Der Standpunkt des alten Materialismus ist die bürgerliche Gesellschaft, der Standpunkt des neuen die menschliche Gesellschaft oder die gesellschaftliche Menschheit.

54 For the play with 'anschauende' and 'Anschauung' see above, note 11 on Thesis 1.

55 This *could* also be translated 'bourgeois society' (= capitalist society) as often in Marx. But in the present context there is not much doubt that 'civil society' is correct.

56 See especially sec. 1 of Marx's Introduction to the *Grundrisse* (The Pelican translation) pp. 83ff.

57 For many stimulating pages on the political economy of subject-object epistemology see the (execrably written) work by R. W. Müller, *Geld und Geist. Zur Entstehungsgeschichte von Identitäts bewuBtsein und Rationalität seit der Antike* (Frankfurt/New York 1977) See also the next note.

58 In Thesis 1 Marx pointed out that classical German idealism had taken up the factor of activity, practice, missing in traditional materialism, but did so in a mystified way. In fact the same idealism took up the *social* factor missing in traditional materialism but again in a mystified way (Kant's transcendental unity of apprecep tion, Hegel's 'Geist' etc.). On Kant in this regard see Bodo v. Greiff, *Gesellschafts-*

form und Erkenntnisform. Zum Zusammenhang von wissenschaftlicher Erfahrung und gesellschaftlicher Entwicklung (Frankfurt/New York 1976), pp. 89f. and the work referred to in the preceding note.

59 Die Philosophen haben die Welt nur verschieden *interpretiert*, es kömt drauf an, sie zu *verändern*.

60 A fuller commentary would point to a similar judgement on Hegel. See the *1844 Manuscripts*, MECW, III, pp. 331f.

61 See *The German Ideology*, MECW, V, pp. 30, 57f.

62 *Philosophy of Right*, Preface, *ad fin.*

63 See *1844 Manuscripts*, MECW, III, pp. 302, 312. *The Holy Family*, MECW, IV, p. 82.

64 *The : German Ideology*, MECW, V, p. 55 note.

65 Karl Korsch is good on this. See his *Three Essays on Marxism* (London 1971), especially pp. 68–71.

66 Lenin put the preceding points in a passage in an early work: The objectivist speaks of the necessity of a given historical process; the materialist gives an exact picture of the given social-economic formation and of the antagonistic relations to which it gives rise. When demonstrating the necessity of a given series of facts, the objectivist always runs the risk of becoming an apologist for these facts: the materialist discloses the class contradictions and in so doing defines his standpoint. The objectivist speaks of 'insurmountable historical tendencies'; the materialist speaks of the class which 'directs' the given economic system, giving rise to such and such forces of counteraction by other classes. Thus, on the one hand, the materialist is more consistent than the objectivist, and gives profounder and fuller effect to his objectivism. He does not limit himself to speaking of the necessity of a process, but ascertains exactly what social-economic formation gives the process its content, exactly what class determines this necessity. . . . On the other hand, materialism includes partisanship, so to speak, and enjoins the direct and open adoption of the standpoint of a definite social group in any assessment of events.' 'The economic content of Narodism (etc.)', *Collected Works*, I (Moscow 1963), pp. 400f.

67 Preface to Shakespeare: The Yale edition of the *Works of Samuel Johnson*, VII (New Haven and London 1968), p. 103.

2 *Materialism and Explanation in the Human Sciences*

ANDREW COLLIER

I hope in this essay to show the distinctions and connections between some of the uses of the word 'materialism' in Marxist thought; to clarify its central use in laying down and justifying some necessary conditions of an adequate explanation in the human sciences; and to show the practical importance of these positions.

Marxists describe themselves as materialists, their philosophy as 'dialectical materialism' and their theory of history as 'historical materialism'. It has often been held – for example by Stalin, though the notion is both older and more widespread than Stalinism as a political phenomenon – that dialectics is a method and materialism a result (or sometimes, a world-view; the latter term is anyway ambiguous between a substantive doctrine about what the world is like – which then appears in contrast to a 'method' by which we choose to investigate things – and a *prise de position*, itself without epistemic justification).

Against this conception, I hold that the status of dialectics and of materialism is that both are verified by the development of scientific knowledge. Dialectics – 'the study of contradiction *in the very essence of objects*' (Lenin, *Collected Works*, XXXVIII, pp. 253–4) – is shown to have or to lack application in the case of each science separately; and although I see no *a priori* objection to a dialectics of nature, I know of only two sciences which require dialectics (that is, which reveal contradictions – in a non-vacuous sense – in their objects): namely, historical materialism and psychoanalysis.[1]

Materialism on the other hand is verified by the development of science in general, and has the status of a group of very general propositions about the sciences and their objects. I think this is also Engels' view – hence his appeal to the history of the sciences as the vindication of his broader philosophical position. For example 'The real unity of the world consists in its materiality and this is proved ... by a long and wearisome development of philosophy and natural science'. (*Anti-Dühring* pp. 58). 'With each epoch-making discovery even in the sphere of natural science [materialism] has to change its form; and after history also was subjected to materialistic treatment, here also a new avenue of development has opened' (*Ludwig Feuerbach* ch.2). On the status of such arguments from the history of science to materialist philosophical positions, see note 14 below. (Needless to say, I am also rejecting another formulation of Stalin's: that historical materialism is merely the application to the phenomena of society of the principles of dialectical materialism. It would be more accurate to say that dialectical materialism is the result of applying a historical materialist analysis to the phenomenon of science and its relation to ideology.)[2]

Philosophically speaking, Marxism is straightforward materialism. The qualification 'dialectical' is not in any sense a reservation about materialism, that is a concession to idealism.[3] It simply marks a resistance to a certain ideological tendency which denies the scientificity of disciplines which concern themselves with contradictions in the dialectical sense.

Materialism is often defined as the primacy of existence over consciousness, or of being over thinking, or of matter over mind. These deceptively simple formulations tend to obscure the fact that there are three related but logically independent doctrines comprising Marxist materialism.

The first, which I shall call 'ontological materialism', is the most familiar sense of the term 'materialism' to non-Marxist philosophers, at least in the English-speaking world. This is a doctrine about the relations between the real-objects of the various sciences, and more specifically between those of the natural sciences on the one hand and the human sciences on the other. It asserts the unilateral dependence of the latter upon the former. This is not, it must be stressed, a doctrine about the relation between the sciences themselves –

that is, it is not reductionism[4]; it concerns only the realities of which these sciences yield knowledge. This has been expressed by my friend Mike Westlake (in an unpublished paper) in the following way:

> The real-object of physics is existentially prior to those of the other sciences. These latter are conceived to be dependent modes of materiality. Their relation to the independent mode, the real-object of physics, may be expressed as: existential dependence and essential independence, and to each other as: existential and essential independence.

(The term 'physics' is used here to refer to the natural sciences generally. The other sciences referred to are historical materialism and psychoanalysis.)

The expression 'essential independence' here indicates that the dependent modes are known through sciences using concepts which are different from and irreducible to those of the natural sciences. The existential dependence of instances of the dependent modes of materiality on instances of the independent mode, is illustrated by the examples of the relation of the meaning of a book to the book as a physical object, and the value of a commodity to the commodity as a physical object[5]. Of this relation, Mike Westlake says:

(1) The existence of an instance of the dependent mode presupposes the existence of an instance of the independent mode; but not *vice versa*.

(2) Any modification of the dependent mode necessarily entails (presupposes) a modification of the independent mode; but not *vice versa*.

(3) A single instance of the dependent mode is 'represented by' (correlated with) an infinite number of instances of the independent mode; but a single instance of the independent mode can 'represent' (be correlated with) no more than one instance of the dependent mode.

So this essay which I have written could not exist as a set of meanings unless it had some physical existence – say, certain marks in black ink on white paper. I cannot alter the essay as a set of meanings without altering these ink marks. While the set of ink marks stays the same, the meaning stays the same. Yet I could have written precisely the same essay in blood, or scratched it in runes on the wall of Bangor Cathedral, or recorded it on a tape, without altering the meaning one jot or tittle.

The human and semiotic sciences then are genuine sciences with their own specific objects; they can formulate laws and describe and explain processes which occur in accordance with those laws, and they do so with concepts specific to themselves, not those of the physical sciences. Yet one cannot conceive of these processes occurring 'disembodied'. In the case most familiar in English-speaking discussions of materialism: one cannot conceive of an alteration in a person's thoughts or mood without a physiological change taking place in that person's brain.

The second part of Marxist materialism can be called epistemological materialism. It states the relation of human knowledge in general to its objects. It can be formulated in two propositions: that everything can be made the object of scientific knowledge, and that such knowledge is independent of its subject. This is the aspect of materialism to which Lenin's remarks (in *Materialism and Empirio-Criticism*) about the *philosophical* sense of 'matter' point; and such recent Marxist thought as accepts this doctrine often tends to treat it as the whole of Marxist materialism.

The third doctrine I shall call 'explanatory materialism'; It is a theory about what counts as a good explanation in science, and is an answer to questions which arise specifically in the human sciences; it is asserted first of all in historical materialism, but I believe it is valid in other human sciences as well. It is this materialist notion of explanation which is what led Marx to call his theory of history 'the *materialist* conception of history' (historical materialism), and not merely the fact that he was claiming scientific status for this theory.

It is often alleged by Marxists that a given putative explanation in a social science is or is not materialist. It is not always clear what this means, though it generally has something to do with the status of material production as the base in relation to the ideologico-political superstructure. It is one aim of this essay to make some steps towards understanding how this characterization ought to be used and why it is important.

First I want to look at the relations between the three materialisms. I hope to show thereby that they are all integral parts of Marxism. I have said that they are logically independent, that is it is possible without inconsistency to assert all three, or to assert any one or two of them while denying the other two or one. Let me elaborate.

(1) Does epistemological materialism entail ontological materialism? If so, then (assuming idealism and materialism to exhaust the possibilities in each field) an ontological idealist would be logically committed to epistemological idealism. There have been many philosophers[6] who have been committed to ontological idealism and 'realism' (or epistemological materialism). So it must be asked whether a coherent version of this position can be constructed.

Its coherence might be contested along the following lines: If the ontological idealist claims that *ideas* are the ultimate constituents of reality, he must be asked whether these ideas exist only in some mind, or independently of any mind. If they are said to be mind-dependent, them 'knowledge' must be invented rather than discovered, and we are back in an epistemologically idealist position. If on the other hand the ideas are said to exist outside any mind, it is not clear in what sense they are ideas. Either there is an incoherence here, or the word 'idea' is being used to refer to some aspect of material reality, and the idealism becomes merely a verbal trick. In that case, no coherent idealist ontology can exist without an idealist epistemology.

But I think that in fact there is one very clear case of an idealist ontology that does not fall to the above objections, namely that of Berkeley. It may seem paradoxical to claim that his idealism relates primarily to ontology, if its essence is seen as '*esse est percipi*'. But in the first place, Berkeley held that the essence of 'spirits' is to perceive and to act, and in the second, what they perceive is not up to them. The function of God in Berkeley's philosophy is not to keep watching the tree in the quad (Berkeley already anticipates the later phenomenalist idea of the permanent possibility of sensations as an answer to that 'problem' – the problem what it *means to say* that there is a trace in the quad.) Where God is indispensible to Berkeley is in the account of the *causation* of our perceptions, given that we don't choose them, and that for Berkeley, only 'spirits', conscious selves, can be causes (a doctrine, by the way, that one still encounters in critics of Freud, who accuse him of attributing action to unconscious ideas, when 'only people can act'.) In the last analysis then, the essence of Berkeley's idealism is this: that he held that causation implies the activity of a conscious causing agent. Everything is the product of mind, but there is no question of *knowledge* producing its own object.

Epistemological idealism in its modern forms – the idea that reality is 'a unity of the given and the constructed' (in Hegel's phrase; or in plain English, a half-truth), and romantic epistemophobia – are probably no older than Kant. It is to these that epistemological materialism as defined above is opposed.

(2) Ontological materialism is quite compatible with a pragmatic-relativistic (and therefore anti-materialist) theory of knowledge. Indeed it has often been held to entail such a theory of knowledge, by those (including some Marxists) who see any causal account of an idea as vitiating its objective validity. The argument is that if all ideas are mere products of objective processes there is no guarantee of their validity as ideas about the real world, and they can be judged only in terms of the function they serve in those (biological, psychological or social) processes. I think this argument can be shown to be incorrect (see for instance David Wiggins' paper 'Freedom, Knowledge, Belief and Causality' in *Knowledge and Necessity*), but the combination of views involved (as opposed to the alleged relations of support between them) does not seem to generate any inconsistencies (unless of course it is claimed that this view is objectively true, in which case a *tu quoque* argument applies).

(3) Epistemological materialism manifestly does not rule out idealist theories of history and society, provided these theories have the *form* of objective science. Part of the point of epistemological materialism is its indifference to the content of the sciences, leaving each science free to discover the nature of its own real object. Once again, this is Lenin's point that if physicists redefine matter, such a redefinition would have no implications for the *philosophical* concept of

matter; conversely, philosophy has no right to legislate as to
how each science should define its own object. And if a
particular scientific theory is incorrect, that in itself does not
make it an idealist theory, any more than a Catholic who
doesn't live according to his beliefs is really a Protestant. One
could quite consistently believe that ideology is determinant
in the last instance in the history of human societies, while
holding a materialist theory of knowledge.

(4) Likewise, ontological materialism does not rule out
idealist theories of history. Perhaps the orthodox view of
history among non-Marxist materialists is that there can be
no science of history because there are no laws of history;
whatever is physically possible could happen in history.[7] Or
again, it could be held that it is ideas that make history, without it being denied that ideas can exist only in the thinking
brain.

(5) Now it must be asked whether the explanatory materialism of Marx's conception of history entails epistemological
materialism. This issue (and that of the ontological implications of historical materialism) stands closer to the centre of
Marxist theory; Marx and his successors have generally only
called on the other materialist principles insofar as this was
necessary in defence of historical materialism. One idealist
line of attack on Marxism has been the claim that human
activity cannot (or should not) be made the object of objective
science. This is perhaps the dominant form of idealism in the
twentieth century: the Canute-like posture which says to the
sciences 'Thus far shalt thou come and no further' when they
touch on human experience and activity. Generally some
form of non-objective pseudo-science is contrived as a
substitute. In this way, this epistemophobia combines with
the other aspect of idealist epistemology, the idea of theory as
the expression of its subject rather than the knowledge of its
object.

But although such a view can be used against historical
materialism by challenging its claim to objectivity, it has
often been held in conjunction with it, for example by
Gramsci and Lukacs, at least in their earlier periods, and by
much of the 'New Left'. Although this conjunction of views
has dangerous political consequences[8], it is not I think

logically incoherent, though it does of course involve seeing historical materialism as the ideology of the most advanced class rather than as a science in the strict sense. This in turn leaves the question why the proletariat should adopt a revolutionary politics rather than a reformist one without any answer but that fool's refuge 'commitment'; whereas if Marxism is an objective science, justified because it tells it like it is, the rationale of revolutionary politics (at least for a worker) is clear as day: there is no other historically possible route to emancipation.

(6) Now to the most fruitful of all aspects of the articulation of Marxist materialism – the possible implications of explanatory materialism in history for ontological materialism. Once again it is easy to see that the relation is not one of logical entailment. Yet the force of many arguments within the materialist theory of history can only be understood by reference to a materialist ontology.

In this connection let me refer to a passage in Sebastiano Timpanaro's book *On Materialism*. He is arguing that most contemporary Marxists have fallen into idealism; comparing their attitudes to the natural sciences – notably biology – with their use of the base-superstructure model in their historical analyses, he says:

> The position of the contemporary Marxist seems at times like that of a person living on the first floor of a house, who turns to the tenant of the second floor and says: 'You think you're independent, that you support yourself by yourself? You're wrong! Your apartment stands only because it is supported on mine, and if mine collapses, yours will too'; and on the other hand to the ground floor tenant: 'What are you pretending? That you support and condition me? What a wretched illusion! The ground floor exists only insofar as it is the ground floor to the first floor. Or rather, strictly speaking, the real ground floor is the first floor, and your apartment is only a sort of cellar, to which no real existence can be assigned. To tell the truth, the relations between the Marxist and the second floor tenant have been perceptibly improved for some time, not because the second-floor tenant has recognized his own 'dependence', but because the Marxist has reduced his pretensions considerably, and has come to admit that the second floor is very largely autonomous from the first, or else that the two apartments 'support each other'. But the contempt for the inhabitant of the ground floor has become increasingly pronounced. *(On Materialism pp. 44–5)*

This metaphor suggests that ontological materialism – the
dependence of the objects of social sciences on those of natural
sciences – and explanatory materialism in history (the base-
superstructure model) are analogous parts of a sort of 'chain
of being'. This is not quite correct, though its correction
would give no comfort to those Timpanaro is criticizing. For
Marxists have always admitted that the superstructure has
effects on the base, and is necessary for the reproduction of the
base, whereas the dependence of social reality on biological
reality is absolute and unilateral.

But what is correct and important in Timpanaro's position
is firstly the place he gives to biology, which tends to be
treated by Marxists as something of a Cinderella among the
sciences, no doubt in reaction to the ideological use made of it
by those ethologists who try to explain what goes on in concrete human societies directly in terms of biological instincts.
It is worth nothing that biological reality is an ontologically
dependent mode in relation to physico-chemical reality, and
that the objects of all social or human sciences are ontologically dependent on it. When we say 'man thinks with his
brain', it should be remembered that the brain is situated in
biological reality, not merely in physico-chemical.

Secondly there is Timpanaro's insistence that biology is not
(to change the metaphor) a ladder which history climbs and
then throws away, but something which continues to produce
effects in social, cultural and psychological reality. In fact
there are two very different ways in which it does so, and
perhaps the main weakness in Timpanaro's extremely re-
freshing book is that this difference is not adequately stressed.
On the one hand, events occur governed by the laws of biology
(and of other natural sciences) which have effects on the
course of history – for example plagues, famines, earth-
quakes, early deaths of politically significant individuals (such
as Lenin). Some of these events are generated quite outside
the social processes of history, yet they intervene in those
processes, sometimes crucially. Incidentally, this fact is
enough to dispel the myth of 'historical inevitability' without
the aid of Popper's ingenious arguments, and certainly without any reference to 'free will'.

But these 'accidents' are not the only ways in which 'nature' affects 'history'. It also *founds* the most basic and general laws of history, though these remain laws of *history*, not of biology. It is sometimes said that what makes Marxism 'dialectical' and 'revolutionary' is that it rejects the idea that any categories pertaining to human societies are applicable for all time – all things must pass. But of course Marx held that there *are* certain invariant features of all possible human societies – production, for instance. Certainly historical materialism would not apply to a society which did not have to produce. But the necessity to produce is determined by the laws of biology, not those of history. And this highly concrete necessity is the foundation of some of the most basic and abstract laws of history.[9]

Just as the applicability of historical materialism depends on the existence of beings which must produce, in ways not instinctually determined, in order to live, so the applicability of psychoanalysis depends on the presence of a sexual instinct with a certain degree of plasticity and of insistence, and on the necessary dependence of the child on adults throughout a prolonged infancy, as well as on certain anatomical features of sexual differentiation. The fact that the crucial instinct in Freudian theory is one which has a somatic source and aim, gives that theory a distinct advantage over the Jungian, Adlerian, existential and cultural schools of 'psychoanalysis', for which the determinant force has no such 'materialist' credentials. Both these theories then (those of Marx and Freud) rest on certain biologically determined characteristics of the human species; both also presuppose the possession of language by mankind, which itself presumably has a biological basis in the complexity of the human brain. The ontological relations between biological, psychological, linguistic and social realities, and their origin, are questions for the theory of evolution.

It is noteworthy that whenever Marx wanted to defend his historial-materialist thesis that the structure constituted by the fores and relations of material production is determinant in the last instance in social development, he did so by reference to biological facts – in the words of the old workers' song 'As man is only human, he must eat before he can think.' So that it is precisely the point of contact between the human

sciences and their biological foundation – the presence of
needs, with definite ranges of variation in means to satisfaction and possibilities of mediation through signs – which is
the foundation of the determination in the last instance by a
specific element – the 'material' element – within the objects
of the human sciences. It is thus to ontological materialism
that Marx appeals in order to justify a materialist theory of
historical explanation.[10] As I have said, the realtion between
these two materialisms is not one of entailment. Rather it is as
if Marx is saying:

> Let us keep our feet on the ground; starting from biologically given
> facts, we can begin to explain the general structures and possibilities
> of human societies. That way we will avoid taking the effect for the
> cause and taking the complex products (real or mythical) of specific
> societies ('the world of the spirit', 'the autonomous individual')
> for the foundation of all society.[11]

It will be seen that this approach has far-reaching consequences for the structure of explanation in the human
sciences. To this end it is necessary to discuss some of the
political uses of explanatory materialism in the human
sciences; I shall then return to the point arrived at above, to
discuss its relation to these uses. It will also emerge that
materialism has important practical implications – an idea
that Marxists have tended to shy away from because of the
vulgar misuse of the word to mean the desire to accumulate
worldly goods. The practical sense of materialism involves not
only the rejection of goals alien to human happiness, but the
understanding that we are creatures of need, dependent on
nature and society outside ourselves, who must therefore
acquire collective power over the objects of need. Materialism
is crucial to Marxism because it shows the inescapability of
politics. It gives the lie to the 'valiant fellow (who) had the
idea that men were drowned in water only because they were
possessed with the idea of gravity' (*The German Ideology*,
preface). But I am anticipating.

When Marx first propounded historical materialism it stood
in obvious contrast to three other views about history: (a) the
'Grand Design' theory as exemplified by Hegel and by some

theological perspectives on history; that is the idea that there is either an immanent teleology or the purpose of a transcendent being working itself out in history, and that this is the ultimate explanation of historical events. (b) the commonsensical view of history as the cumulative effect of many individual purposes. It is admittedly a little more contentious to say that Marx was rejecting this view, as both he and Engels spoke at times as if (i) history is the resultant of the interplay of many purposes, though this resultant is not necessarily in agreement with any of them; and (ii) when socialism has eliminated the blind force of the world market as a way of arriving at this resultant, history will become a matter of the conscious purposes of a collectivity. Now these two propositions are not actually false, but they can be quite misleading for reasons which will become clear shortly. Here I will merely note two mistakes to be avoided.

In an article in the *New Reasoner*, no. 8, Alasdair MacIntyre says: ' "Men make their own history, but . . . " This phrase echoes through the Marxist classics. The political aim of Marxists is to liquidate that "but".' If he had finished the quote, he could not have made that comment on it, for the point is that men make history *on the basis of conditions not of their own choosing*, and that is a fact that cannot be liquidated. When it is added that men are the products of their material and social conditions, the other mistake – that which is encapsulated in the phrase 'the self-production of man' – is also exposed for what it is. Immediately after speaking of the collective control of social forces in socialist society, Marx and Engels issue this warning:

> Now this view can be expressed again in speculative-idealistic, that is fantastic, terms as 'self-generation of the species' ('society as the subject'), and thereby the consecutive series of interrelated individuals connected with each other can be conceived as a single individual, which accomplishes the mystery of generating itself. It is clear here that individuals certainly make *one another*, physically and mentally, but do not make themselves. (*The German Ideology* pp.55–6)

The final view excluded by Marx's formulations is (c) the notion that ideas (rather than the forces and relations of

production, and the class struggle generated by the contradictions between them) are the motors of history. One aspect
of his rejection of this view is that historical movements are
judged not in terms of their self-images and subjective inten-
tions, but of their objective causes and effects. So that one is
not interested in whether Cromwell was a good Calvinist,
Robespierre a good Rousseauite or Mao Tse-Tung a good
Marxist, but in what class forces they represented and what
the effect of their policies has been in terms of class
relations.

Appeals are often made to explanatory materialism in
political arguments in Marxist circles. Explanations of political disasters in terms of conspiracy or betrayal are rejected in
the name of this principle; views of ideology which see it as
arising from the propaganda of the media are criticized on the
grounds that ideas are not produced by ideas but by social
conditions. In practice, many socialists overestimate the
historical effectivity of socialist ideology, while having a
correct assessment of other ideologies, but this too is inconsistent with Marxist theory. To give two examples: in discussions of Russia in the 1920s it is often alleged that the
erosion of proletarian democracy and the substitution of the
Party for the class was rendered historically innocuous (that
is, did not lead to the emergence of a new class) by virtue of the
fact that the Party was guided by a correct Marxist theory (or
alternatively, that this substitution would have been harmless
had the Party not deviated theoretically); yet for a historical
materialist, no amount of correct theory on the part of the
elite can restore power to the workers once it has passed from
their hands. Secondly, much has been made in Cuba and
China of the idea that material incentives for work are being or
could and should be replaced by moral incentives. It seems to
me that this idea too is incompatible with historical materialism.

Now what these negative implications of historical materialism have in common is rejection of any explanation in terms
of agency, in favour of explanation in terms of objective laws,
which can also explain the phenomenon of agency[12]. This I
think takes us to the heart of the antagonism between idealism
and materialism: idealism defends and elaborates theoreti-

cally the feeling (which dominates commonsensical explanations) that one has explained an event when one has traced it to an agent. If explanation were a merely subjective matter – a matter of producing satisfaction in the mind of an enquirer – one could hardly find a better explanation than agency; but of course for science, agency is precisely what has to be explained. Every scientist knows this and it is in this sense that scientists are spontaneously materialist. The issue between idealist and materialist explanation can now be seen to be the basis of the epistemological and ontological issues as well. Idealist epistemology asserts that we do not discover laws in nature but put them into the phenomena, hence the agency of the knowing subject is supposed to explain the laws. Ontological idealism traces laws of nature back to a law-giving agent (for example in the argument from design, or in theories of history or psychology which see laws as 'reified praxis'). As already seen, the essence of Berkeley's idealism was not *esse est percipi*, but his assertion that only agents could cause. It might even be said that subjection to laws is the criterion of the materiality of a putative reality, reference to agency the criterion of ideality. Of course, the materialist does not deny that agency has some kind of being, any more than the idealist denies that laws of nature do.[13] The question is rather, What explains what? And this is the question, not only when one is concerned with materialism and idealism as explanatory principles in the human sciences, but also at the levels of epistemology and ontology.

Now I do not believe that materialist and idealist notions of explanation can achieve any sort of peaceful co-existence by relegating the former to science and the latter to common sense; the task of materialist philosophy is to drive idealism from its home territory of common sense. It must do this because idealism – even when confined to commonsense discourse – has effects both in politics and in human relationships.

A fine example of the political use of idealism is Sir Keith Joseph's speech on the decadence of contemporary Britain, which must have struck a note on the keyboard of every petty-bourgeois imagination. Let me quote from it a little:

We have to get economics back into proportion, as one aspect of politics, important but never really the main thing

over the years this auction (that is, rival economic promises at elections – A.C.) has raised expectations which cannot be satisfied, generated grievances and discontents

He puts forward, apparently as a political programme:

... respect for other people and for law, the welfare of young people, the state of family life, the moral welfare of the people, cultural values, public-spiritedness ... , national defence, the tone of national life.

The economic situation is not an independent variable

If we ask: Independent of what? his answer is:

economics is deeply shaped by values, by the attitudes towards work, thrift, ethics, public spirit.

we were taught that crime, violence, wife-beating, child-beating were the result of poverty

(He is of course implying that poverty is no longer with us). He has his own base-superstructure model:

the family and civilized values. Those are the foundation on which the nation is built.

The whole of explanatory idealism is there; it is a consistent world-view. Sir Keith Joseph recognizes – as his liberal opponents do not – that political, collective solutions to social problems are *alternatives* to the moral solutions which he is advocating. These political solutions, he is claiming, have been tried and have failed; it is time to return to moral ones. I don't question that his moral conclusion follows from his factual premiss – which however is false. But so far it looks as if his ideas are political only in a negative sense – that he sees the moralization of people as a preferable alternative to political action for their equality and welfare. Yet there *is* a political programme here, as can be seen from proposals such as that politicians should 'deal with' the moral welfare of the people, and his extraordinary notion – used in connection with his tribute to Mary Whitehouse – of 'protecting adolescents from permissiveness'. These clearly indicate political action for ideological ends – the enforcement of morals. Though he tells us that freedom begins with self-discipline, he obviously believes that self-discipline begins with external discipline in the family and the school, and that political power must be used to enforce this.

Here can be seen a fundamental political antagonism which logically rests on a fundamental disagreement about the explanation of social phenomena. There is a problem in that the economic system is not meeting people's expectations. Sir Keith Joseph's solution: the aim of political action must be to enforce self-discipline, resignation, hard work, and personal responsibility, so as to cut expectations down to a size that the economic system can meet. The socialist solution: the aim of political action must be to transform the relations and increase the forces of production, so that these expectations can be met.

The 'reason' for this disagreement – I am speaking ideologically – is that Sir Keith Joseph explains the original problem in terms of agency – people have chosen to be selfish, to worship instinct and spontaneity and reject discipline and so on. The Marxist on the other hand explains the problem in terms of the laws governing the economic system – capitalism – and generating contradictions within it. And this system and these laws exist independently of anyone's will.

Now it will be alleged – quite correctly – that the real reason for this political disagreement is that Sir Keith Joseph and the Marxist represent the standpoints of different classes. They do indeed, but the coherence of each view depends on its theoretical basis – an idealist or materialist notion of explanation of social phenomena.

The same ideological conflict occurs at the micro-social level as well. It may be illustrated by the conflict within the work of a writer such as R.D. Laing, between the Freudian explanation of agency in terms of instinctual vicissitudes and the psychic institutions, and the Sartrean notion of 'intelligibility' as resolving 'process into praxis'. I have discussed this at some length in my book on R.D. Laing. Here, I will restrict my remarks to an attack on one commonsense explanatory concept – that of an 'attitude'.

It is generally assumed that an attitude (in one use of the word) is something that can be taken up or laid down at will, like an umbrella, and which is not itself in need of an explanation; at the same time it is seen as explaining behaviour quite satisfactorily. One hears it said: 'It is the attitude you are taking which is causing the trouble'. The implication is generally that the attitude is quite gratuitous. Many motive-words are used in this way; 'everybody knows' why a burglar steals, or a man rapes a woman, or a mother batters her baby: it is out of 'greed' or 'lust' or 'cruelty'. The obviousness of these ready-to-hand explanations enables one to dismiss sociological or psychological explanations without consideration. I recall an incident in *Z-cars* when the sergeant was making fun of a sociologist for thinking that it was bad social conditions which led to crime, along the lines: 'that may be all right in London, but here in Newtown (where, presumably, conditions are different) it won't work. Round here, people are just vicious'.

One does not generally hear such crude arguments from members of the educated classes – unless one includes Sir Keith Joseph – but it is really only the terminology that changes. In would-be liberated circles one often hears that this person is being 'aggressive', that one 'defensive', another is 'on an ego-trip', a fourth 'refuses to let go'. Sometimes these attributions may not be intended to be understood as attitudes in the present sense, but they usually are.

Of course one does not generally attribute these things to oneself; attitudes are things that other people have. That in itself is not an argument against the concept – it may well be possible to be more objective about other people than about oneself. But a genuinely objective explanation of behaviour would concern the past experience, emotional economy and current situation of the individual, and would not use attitude-concepts. (My point is not a Rylean one; I accept character-realism, but I am claiming that the commonsense account of motivation encapsulated in the word 'attitude' is an

idealist one, and is false. It is idealist because attitudes appear
to explain without themselves having an explanation, and
gain this appearance as attributes of a conscious, responsible
'last cause'.)

If it is possible for materialism to conquer even these
darkest heartlands of common sense, I believe it would effect
a complete and altogether desirable revolution in human
relationships; of course, I don't think that this can be brought
about by a 'change of attitude', or by philosophical conviction of the truth of materialism.

But at any rate the idealism—materialism dichotomy is
entirely applicable even at this everyday level. The idealist-in-
the-street accounts for both political discontent and noxious
private behaviour in terms of (a) a set of attitudes, at once
completely comprehensible and completely gratuitous, and
usually disreputable, (b) some kind of 'outside agitators'
appealing to these attitudes (not necessarily left-wing political
agitators; it could be the advertising industry, or 'sex-n-
violence' on the television), and (c) a voluntary choice of self-
indulgence. The materialist-in-the-street will account for the
same phenomena in terms of (a) needs, (b) a reality which
frustrates them, and (c) behaviour which is either an attempt
to change that reality or to come to terms with it.

Now to return to some of the theoretical ends which I left
untied. I have drawn two conclusions about explanatory
materialism in the human sciences—one about its being
grounded in the biological foundation of the human sciences,
and one about its essential point being the notion that the
agency is always an *explanadum*, never an *explanans*. What is
the connection between these two conclusions?

In the first place, the biological foundation of social existence explains why explanatory materialism is true. I do not
mean it is the evidence for explanatory materialism (though
some of Marx's formulations might suggest that, and
evidence being the complex thing that it is, this should not be
dismissed); but it does explain why human social existence is
such that explanatory materialism holds in regard to it. I
might be replied: but this needs no explanation, for agency
could not conceivably be an *explanans*. This may be true
I would not myself be prepared to assert it for all possible

worlds, though I do not think that this is an important concession.[14] The point is that the notion of agency, which the idealists take for an *explanans*, is derived from *this* world, and it can be shown that the phenomenon which it denotes occurs in accordence with laws, which explain it, and which are themselves explained in terms of biological reality. If one carefully averts ones eyes from all that is biological, it is easy to see voluntary execution of conscious purposes – 'praxis', if you like – as the essence of human reality. As soon as one looks at the biologically given raw material of that reality, 'free will' (in the anti-determinist sense – and what else can 'praxis' be if it is not governed by laws?) comes to look as out of place in the human sciences as a werewolf in a zoology textbook.

Here is seen a connection between explanatory and ontological materialism: the laws of historical materialism explain what happens in history, but the laws of biology explain those laws, without replacing them, that is the laws of biology do not themselves explain what happens in history. There must also be a physico-chemical explanation of the laws of biology. Only the laws of physics and the being of something rather than nothing are without explanation. This does not mean that the laws of historical materialism can simply be read off from biological laws. They are discovered as a result of research into the working of human societies. Marx, Engels and Lenin did in fact tend to exaggerate the degree of support given to historical materialism by biological facts. Thus, according to Engels, Marx:

> discovered the simple fact, hitherto concealed by an overgrowth of ideology, that mankind must first of all eat and drink, have shelter and clothing, before it can pursue politics, science, religion, art etc.; and that therefore the production of the immediate material means of subsistence and consequently the degree of economic development attained by a given people or during a given epoch, form the foundation upon which the state institutions, the legal conceptions, the art and even the religious ideas of the people concerned have been evolved, and in the light of which these things must therefore be explained, instead of *vice versa* as had hitherto been the case.

> (Speech at the graveside of Karl Marx)

Similar statements can be found in Lenin's article 'Karl Marx' and in numerous other texts by Engels. This looks as if the whole base-superstructure theory is a logical consequence of the fact that one must eat, which was not exactly discovered by Marx.

But it is noteworthy that Engels' point is about the *direction of explanation*. From the fact that we are in the first place and inescapably creatures of need, for whom consciousness, culture and long-term purposes always come later and are constructed out of the givens of biology, it may follow that these 'higher' things, the loci of agency, must always be explained in terms of the 'lower', the things independent of our will and consciousness. This tells us what sort of explanatory work has to be done; it does not do it for us. Not only does there remain the work of concrete analysis of particular societies; even at the abstract level, laws governing the production of political or ideological effects are not yet touched on by this materialist conclusion as to the *direction* of explanation. Yet it is not empty. It rules out any irreducible teleology, whether holistic (society as an organism with its own purposes) or atomistic (the market as the expression of 'consumer free choice'. Methodological individualism will hardly hold up if the choices of individuals are not seen as somehow irreducible).

Consciousness, agency, and all aspects of social existence which give rise to ideology and appear to idealism as the foundation of social life are actually produced by the interaction of needs which are at the outset biological givens, with the external world. These needs permeate all aspects of human existence, set the limits to human possibilities, and must figure in or be taken for granted by explanations in all the social sciences.

There is one more aspect of explanatory materialism which I would like to note briefly. There are various putative forms of explanation in the human sciences which are distinct from the mechanistic causality of natural science, for example teleological, holistic, structural, functional, etc. explanations. It is for each science to say whether a particular form of explanation has or lacks application in its own area.[15]

But ontological materialism implies that for any explanation to be true, there must be an explanation of the same process under some physical description. It is therefore legitimate to ask, when confronted with a non-mechanistic explanation: 'How does this come about?', where this is understood as an inquiry about the connections between the phenomena figuring in the explanation, to be sketched in such a way that it would in principle be possible to trace the connections as a chain of cause and effect.

This is not a plea for reductionism, but for keeping it in mind that, for example, a structure does not determine its elements or the bearers of positions in it by magic. Magical thinking is not unknown in Marxist literature, as witness the unworked-out use of the notion of representation, in discussions of the class bases of politics. I think any analysis of the political debates in Russia in the 1920s will show that all sides assumed a magical relationship of representation between the Communist Party and the working class, which served as a rationalization for substitutionism and the relegation of the soviets to a nominal role. Trotsky – though 'the best Marxist of his time' – was as deeply mystified as anyone about this.

This idea that the party is somehow essentially and indissolubly bound to the interests of the working class – precluding analysis of the mechanisms by which genuine representation can take place – still has the most profound political effects, and remains the biggest theoretical obstacle to the building of an international socialist movement dedicated to workers' democracy. Jiri Pelikan mentions how this assumption stopped Czechoslovakian Marxists from doubting that the seizure of power by Communist leaders in 1948 established *workers'* power (see Jiri Pelikan: *The struggle for socialism in Czechoslovakia*). At the other end of the Marxist spectrum, the same assumption is behind the ludicrous claim of the Socialist Party of Great Britain that, as it represents the workers, all other parties must be bourgeois.

More recently, in the work of Populantzas, we read about particular parts of the *state apparatus* 'representing' particular classes or fractions of classes – potentially a very fruitful notion if the political and ideological mechanisms whereby the representation of those classes and fractions by those apparatuses are secured, could be demonstrated. But one searches in vain in Poulantzas's books for such a demonstration; one is left with the feeling that no more can be meant than that such apparatuses are manned by individuals originating from the classes in question – a conclusion which Poulantzas could certainly not consistently accept.

I am not proposing that the notion of political representation of economic classes should be scrapped, as do the authors of *Marx's 'Capital' and Capitalism Today*. There are Marxist political analyses in which the requisite concept of mechanisms of representation exists 'in a practical state' (if there were not, Marxist politics would have not one ounce of justification for its claim to be scientific, and we would be back with Owen and Weitling). But the political use of an unexplained notion of representation is too widespread and too dangerous to be left to chance. A similar theoretical and political error lies behind talk of common 'ownership' of the means of production by the workers in countries where there are no institutions through which they can exercise their rights as owners.

Notes

1 'Nature is the test of dialectics' says Engels. *One* meaning of this is that dialectical theory is an empirical hypothesis. True, Engels went on to claim that it had been verified in some natural sciences, and placed great importance on this. But if he is wrong about particular instances, nothing is thereby proved about its applicability in historical materialism. At least he did not give it an *a priori* character.

   Those dialectical materialists who find dialectical contradictions under every stone they turn up inevitably end by either trivializing the dialectic or subjectivizing it.

2 These errors occur in the first two paragraphs of Stalin's essay 'Dialectical and Historical Materialism'. The rest of the essay, despite its schematic and aprioristic nature, has at least the merit of avoiding the crasser mistakes of western idealist Marxism. Needless to say the credit for this should not go to Stalin – whose career as a theoretician grew out of the barrel of a gun – but to the 'authorities' on which he bases himself that is Marx, Engels, Lenin, and probably (unacknowledged for obvious reasons) his victim Bukharin.

3 Though it is true that Marxists recognize a certain relative autonomy and effectivity of mind, and those who use the word 'dialectical' to mean 'two-way' or 'complex' call this recognition 'dialectical'. I find this usage superfluous.

4 There are of course reductionist materialisms, for example 'physicalism' in the philosophy of mind. But Marxism has never been materialist in this sense.

5 Not that the value of a commodity can't fluctuate without alteration to the physical object – it can, as value is a relation not a quality. But in order to have any value, a thing must have use-value, and this is dependent on its physical constitution. This is an instance of a more general phenomenon, which makes it necessary to qualify the third point about the relations between dependent and independent modes. An instance of a dependent mode is defined as what it is by virtue of its relational properties; so that the configuration of ink marks 'pain' signifies suffering if situated in an English sentence, bread if situated in a French one. But point 3 can be saved by adding 'while the relations of the instance of the dependent mode to other such instances remain constant'. This does not trivialize the point; it still excludes the possibility of disembodied changes in the dependent mode as a whole.

6 The most eminent perhaps being Plato. A clear statement of this combination of views by a modern philosopher can be found at the beginning of an essay by McTaggart: 'Ontologically I am an Idealist, since I believe that all that exists is spiritual.... I believe.... that

57

the only substances are selves, parts of selves, and groups of selves or parts of selves.

On the other hand, I should say that epistemologically I was a Realist. I should say that knowledge was a true belief, and I should say that a belief was true when, and only when, it stands in a relation of correspondence to a fact.' ('An ontological idealism' in *Contemporary British Philosophy*, 1924).

7   Remember the story of the Rabbi's answer to the question whether there is a peaceful road to socialism: 'There are two such roads, one natural and one supernatural. The natural one is this: the Archangel Michael could descend from heaven with a fiery sword and transform the capitalists into pillars of salt. The supernatural way is that the capitalists could give up their power without a fight.'

If this answer combines an idealist ontology with a materialist conception of history, our contrary expectation expresses the familiarity of the opposite judgement.

8   It can lead to utopian illusions of revolution by change of consciousness, underestimating the objective strength of the enemy; or it can be used by a tyrannical bureaucracy to justify a Macchiavellian contempt for truth and for scientific freedom.

9   André Glucksmann, in his essay 'A ventriloquist structuralism' (printed in *Western Marxism – A Critical Reader*), accuses Louis Althusser of holding as a metaphysical principle that every practice must have the structure of production. He quotes what Heidegger has written of Marx's materialism, that 'The essence of materialism does not consist in the claim that everything is elementary matter *(Stoff)*, but rather in a metaphysical determination according to which all being appears as the raw material *(Material)* of labour'. (*Letter on Humanism*, quoted p. 310n).

The correct reply to this – though I cannot imagine Althusser assenting to it – would be to point out that one need only appeal to human biology, not to metaphysics, to prove that human activities must have this form.

10   For instance 'The first premise of all human history is, of course, the existence of living human individuals. Thus the first fact to be established is the physical organization of these individuals and their consequent relation to the rest of nature ... (men) begin to distinguish themselves from animals as soon as they begin to *produce* their means of subsistence, a step which is conditioned by their physical organization' (*The German Ideology*, p. 42).

'One thing is clear: the Middle Ages could not live on Catholicism, nor could the ancient world on politics. On the contrary, it is the manner in which they gained their livelihood which explains why in one case politics, in the other case Catholicism, played the chief part' (*Capital* I, p. 176n).

'All that palaver about the necessity of proving the concept of value comes from complete ignorance both of the subject dealt with and of scientific method. Every child knows that a nation which ceased to work, I will not say for a year, but even for a few weeks, would perish. Every child knows, too, that the masses of products corresponding to the different needs require different and quantitatively determined masses of the total labour of society. That this *necessity* of the *distribution* of social labour in definite proportions cannot possibly be done away with by a *particular form* of social production but can only change the *mode* of its *appearance* is self-evident. No natural laws can be done away with.' (Marx, in letter to Kugelmann, 11 July, 1868. *Selected Correspondence*, p. 209). None of this should be taken as meaning that the law of value or the determining role of the economic structure can be *derived from* a materialist ontology; but they are built on foundations which can (see the concluding pages of this essay).

11 The appeals to the temporal priority of nature over history in the classic Marxist texts has its place here. If human consciousness and culture has emerged on the basis of millenia of geological and biological development, it is hard to believe it can suddenly make itself autonomous, let alone the centre of the universe.

Of course, the epistemological idealist will simply deny the premise.

12 'Agency' here in the sense of will, conscious purpose, being a 'responsible agent', with more than a suggestion of the idea of an 'unmoved mover'.

There are other possible uses of the term 'agency', where it can be attributed to anything that has powers to cause certain events under certain conditions; the powers are explained by the structure of the agent. Thus a hydrogen atom has the power, determined by its internal structure, to combine with another hydrogen atom and an oxygen atom to form a molecule of water, just as a men has the power, also determined by his internal structure, to use language. See Bhaskar's *A Realist Theory of Science*. This notion of agency is thoroughly materialist.

13 The expression 'Law of nature' *can* mean a formulation of a law, as part of a scientific discourse. A 'law' in this sense, of course, *is* a human product. But in that case we need another expression to denote the aspect of objective reality which makes a law true, or if you like, that in nature which corresponds to a law. Bhaskar uses the term 'generative mechanism'. It is of course the primacy of generative mechanisms, not of our theories, that the ontological materialist asserts; otherwise he would be committed to an idealist epistemology.

14 It is of the essence of science to discover causal laws governing objective processes, and to explain the phenomena in terms of them. All three materialisms therefore have the status of something like 'conditions of the possibility' of science. But that doesn't make them *a priori* truths, as the idea that science is *not* possible isn't contradictory – merely false.

The roots of idealism must, I take it, be sought closer to home than in the philosophical disciplines of epistemology and ontology: it is

60   Andrew Collier

initially a resistance (in the Freudian sense) to scientific explanation in the human world.

15 Though of course some of these forms of 'explanation' may turn out to be idealist alternatives to scientific explanation. For instance, teleological explanation can only be accepted insofar as its non-teleological foundations are demonstrated.

Bibliography

Bhaskar, Roy, *A Realist Theory of Science* (Hassocks 1978).

Collier, Andrew, *R. D. Laing: the philosophy and politics of psychotherapy* (Hassocks 1977).

Cutler, Hirst, Hindess and Hussain, *Marx's Capital and Capitalism Today* (London 1977).

Engels, Friedrich, *Anti-Dühring* (Moscow 1969); 'Ludwig Feuerbach' in *Selected Works* (London 1968); 'Speech at the graveside of Karl Marx'.

Glucksmann, André, 'A ventriloquist structuralism' in *Western Marxism: a Critical Reader* (London 1977).

Joseph, Sir Keith, Speech in Birmingham, reported in '*The Observer*' 20 October 1974.

Lenin, Vladimir, *Materialism and Empirio-Criticism* (Moscow 1947); *Philosophical Notebooks (Collected Works XXXVIII)* (London 1961).

MacIntyre, Alasdair, 'Notes from the moral wilderness' in *The New Reasoner*, no. 8.

MacTaggart, J. Ellis 'An ontological idealism' in *Contemporary British Philosophy: Personal Statements* (first series) (ed.) J. H. Muirhead (London 1924).

Marx, Karl *Capital*, I (Harmondsworth 1976).

Marx, Karl and Engels, Friedrich, *The German Ideology*, pt. 1, C. J. Arthur (ed.) (London 1970); *Selected Correspondence* (Moscow 1965).

Pelikan, Jiri, 'The struggle for socialism in Czechoslovakia' in *Revolution and Class Struggle*, Robin Blackburn (ed.) (London and Hassocks 1977).

Poulantzas, Nicos, *Political Power and Social Classes* (London 1973).

Stalin, Joseph, 'Dialectical and historical materialism', ch. 4 pt. 2, *The History of the Communist Party of the Soviet Union (Bolsheviks)* (Moscow 1941).

Timpanaro, Sebastiano, *On Materialism* (London 1975).

Westlake, Michael, 'The ontology of materialism' (unpublished essay, quoted with the permission of the author).

Wiggins, David, 'Freedom, knowledge, belief and causality' in *Knowledge and Necessity*, Royal Institute of Philosophy lectures, 1968–9 (Hassocks 1970).

3 *Marxism, Materialism and Biology*
KATE SOPER

MAN, said Aristotle, – and Marx saw fit to repeat him – is a
zoon politikon, a social animal.[1] That was some time ago, but
seldom, if ever, for all the disparity of views that have been
promulgated since on the subject of 'what man is', has the
truth of the adage been disputed. One can only infer from this
that, as with all such accepted wisdoms, it is the interpreter
who calls the tune and the appeal of the central theme expressed lies in the ease with which it lends itself to variation.

One clue to the versatility of Aristotle's pronouncement is
that it points in two directions – to a common animal existence
on the one hand, and to a distinguishing social existence on
the other. It speaks of both biology and society, of both nature
and culture; but it does not speak, or at least not explicitly, of
the relations between these apparent antitheses. It is we who
must lend it precision in that respect. For though it would
seem to be the case that man is both a biological and a social
creature, who can no more neglect the claims of the 'natural'
for attention than those of the 'social' in order to reach an
understanding of homo sapiens, the point is how exactly to
interpret such claims. What role to assign to 'nature' and
specifically human biology, on the one hand, and to 'society'
on the other in constituting both human history and the
individuals of that history?

There can be no quick way with this, for while there may be
a *prima facie* plausibility in the notion that the substance of
human history is reached through an addition of natural and
social features, or the substance of the individual is reached
through some combination of biological and social components, there is still the problem of what kind of 'addition' or
'combination' is involved. Moreover, it is questionable
whether the notions of 'addition' and 'combination', implying
as they do some pure existential status that each component

has prior to its union with the other in the constitution of history and the individual – and thus the possibility of separation between 'nature' and 'society' – do not themselves rest on mistaken conceptions of the 'natural' and the 'social'. So it is both these terms and the relations posited between them that stand in need of further examination.

I shall be particularly concerned here with what historical materialism and Marxist epistemology imply for our understanding of the natural – social relationship. I shall discuss and criticize the ways in which Marxism invites us to neglect and underestimate the role of nature and of biology; but I shall also hope to show in what ways its materialist theory of knowledge suggests an approach to the nature-society relationship that breaks with any view of human culture as the product of an addition or mixture of ontologically separate and antithetical components – those of 'nature' on the one hand, and of 'society' on the other. In place of such a conception I shall argue that human culture comprises a single order in which one never discovers purely 'natural' or purely 'social' elements instantiated concretely, but which can be studied at different levels of abstraction; and I shall argue that it is only in the distinction of a relatively low level of abstraction at which we attempt to conceptualize the presence in human culture of determinations accountable to the structures and properties studied by the more abstract sciences of physics, chemistry and biology, that it is meaningful to talk about something called the 'relationship between nature/biology and society'. This means that in an overall way I shall be arguing that one must substitute epistemological distinctions which differentiate between levels at which one has knowledge of what is a single ontological unity for a view which regards the 'biological' or 'social' as designating distinct kinds of existence within human culture.

In order to exemplify this position I propose to take up certain 'challenges' that have questioned the adequacy of the Marxist, or purportedly Marxist, account of the natural-social relationship, and therefore directly invite consideration of what does indeed constitute a materialist approach to that issue. Some of these 'challenges' have been expressly formulated, while others are merely implicit in the form and activities of various contemporary political movements; but they can all be said to centre on the theme of Marxism's neglect of biology.

Now it is indeed true that for some time now Marxists have been suspicious of biology, as if merely to entertain its claim to attention were to be implicated in the atrocities of vulgar materialism. No doubt in the heyday of biologism such fastidiousness was a sign of health. At any rate it was understandable. But the fact is that in its zeal to escape the charge of biological reductionism, Marxism has tended to fall prey to an antithetical form of reductionism, which in arguing the dominance of social over natural factors literally spirits the biological out of existence altogether.

I suggest that in theoretical controversies such as this, which are presided over by a *fear* on the one hand (in this case of biologism) and a *repression* (of the object of concern, namely, biology) on the other, we must suspect a failure to confront the truth. However, it is not my intention here to chronicle, let alone psychoanalyze, Marxism's theoretical obsessions and evasions on this issue, but merely to mention some ways in which the real effects of an actual and ongoing relationship between biological and social factors – effects which testify to the indissolubility of one set of factors into the other – are lived and felt politically; hence to argue the political relevance of a considered and non-evasive investigation of this relationship.

The 'challenges'
I shall merely list these here and then return to each of them in more detail later. In the first place, then, there is the feminist challenge, which is implicit in the autonomy of the Womens Movement as a politics separate from or only tangential to Marxism, and which when rendered explicit rebukes Marxism for its continued neglect of the fact that the history of society is not only a history of class division but also a history of sexual division. The patriarchal order which embodies the latter, is, it is argued, no less oppressive in its effects than is economic exploitation; why, then, should the latter be allowed to play the role of principle *explanans* in any account of social development? What this questions is the

adequacy of historical materialism as an explanation of history, or at least the adequacy of any explanation that purports to reduce all social divisions to class divisions and refuses to understand the specificity of sexual oppression.

Similar arguments have been voiced in regard to racial oppression: here again there is felt to be a certain glibness in Marxist explanations which abstract from the particular features and significance of racial politics. Given, then, that Marxism has tended to bypass or to provide economistic accounts of sexual and racial conflict, it is not surprising to find the claims of the latter to attention have been asserted, at least by some factions engaged in these struggles, as if female and racial emancipation were in competition with rather than integral to economic emancipation. It is a short step thence to insist upon the primacy of sexual or racial determinants and to regard the Marxist identification of history with the history of class struggle as party to a history of male and white supremacy to the extent that it serves to obscure those 'other histories' of sexual and racial conflict. I believe, in fact, that this is essentially a self-stultifying position to adopt on these issues, and I shall hope to show why; but it is precisely because any attempt to do so must proceed by way of rather than at the expense of a consideration of the relations between biology and society that they are raised here.

Secondly, there is the challenge contained in the demand for a so-called 'theory of needs'. The emergence of this concept, and of the whole terrain of considerations included within it, constitutes a major political impetus to re-opening debate on the question of the biological – or, more largely, natural – as opposed to social determinants upon human development. It has for some time been realized among Marxists[2] that the traditional faith in the development of the productive forces to overcome all obstacles to the formation of an authentic socialist society must be reconsidered in the light of contemporary world ecological resources and in view of capitalism's capacity to determine the forms of appropriation of these resources in accordance with the maintenance of its relations of production. This means that a socialist politics must question its former reliance on the inheritance of an expropriated capitalist technology, and along with that the whole system of needs to which it has given rise, and which, it has been assumed, a socialist economy would continue in large part to meet and even to expand upon. In other words, 'rational' alternatives to a capitalist mode of production cannot simply depend upon changes in economic ownership, even if such changes were not merely nominal but constituted a genuine transfer of control over production, but must also be concerned with the entire structure and goals of the material – technical appropriation of nature in the satisfaction of human needs.

It is clear that this question cannot even be discussed let alone resolved without reference to the physico-chemical structure of inorganic matter and to the physical and psychological character of the human beings who are both the agents of production and the subjects of consumption. To argue this is not to argue that either natural resources or human needs can be treated as ahistoric givens possessed of an autonomous determination that is unaffected by the process of social production, but rather to recall attention to the fact that all social production is a process of material production and thus subject to specific material determinations, even where its prime impetus is the production of exchange-value. The difference between a market and a planned economy lies in the degree of directness with which the latter takes account of these determinations and thus replaces *a posteriori* adjustment to them by *a priori* control over them. In a planned economy use-value is no longer merely the inevitable byproduct of the accumulation of capital, but the direct object of production; thus the form that it takes and the role that it plays in both shaping and meeting human requirements become the subject of political decision rather than the effect of economic dictate. What the natural world is physically and who we are biologically and psychologically are then no longer subordinate factors but become predominant in social production to the point where the opposition between the direct impact of 'economic' factors and the indirect effect of 'anthropological' needs is in principle dissolved. But if one is to speak in this connexion of a resolution of an opposition or contradiction between 'natural' and 'economic' determinants it is all the more important to understand the character of this contradiction and its location.

Thirdly, there is the challenge to Marxism to provide a theory of the 'person' or 'individual'. The trouble with this one is that it can be interpreted in a number of differing ways not all of which constitute authentic challenges in the sense that they entertain the possibility of a Marxist reply; some of them are rather designed to expose the errors of its doctrine as a whole. I am not concerned here with Marxism's alleged failure to provide an account of the 'role of the individual in history'[3] but with the accusation that Marxism fails to provide an account of the particularity of the person or a 'theory of personality'. But there can be different formulations, even of that claim, which need to be distinguished.

Many readers will no doubt associate it with Sartre's well-known objection that Marxism can tell us that Valéry is petit bourgeois but not why every petit bourgeois is not Valéry.[4] Now Sartre's challenge is ambiguous between an open-minded invitation to Marxism and an existentialist rejection of its premises. On the first, more generous interpretation, it would be saying something like this: it is in principle possible for historical materialism in conjunction with other human sciences to provide an account of the individual as a unified product of many determinations; in fact Marxism has tended to offer an economistic account which reduces individuals to their economic and class relations and therefore fails to elaborate upon the many other determinants that produce individual difference within the sameness of those economic and class relations.

On the second interpretation it would be saying something to the effect that Marxism is incapable of accounting for individuality because no matter how many determinations a non-economistic theory might discover as contributing to a person's individuality, these are all *a posteriori* to a pre-existent 'particularity' – a core subjectivity – which consists in the 'absolute freedom' wherein the individual constitutes the self in a free projection of choices. In this conception, individuality, even though subject to innumerable mediations (which Marxism can help to explain) remains an undetermined and therefore unaccountable determinant upon the way in which such mediations will be lived. The subject is preassumed, *a priori*, as the agent of a set of choices and cannot therefore be theorized as a product of determinations external to that subjectivity. If Sartre's demand is that Marxism should know, in the sense of explain, a subjectivity so conceived it is clearly impossible for it to do so, since it ultimately depends on retaining individuality as that which by definition is unknowable and inexplicable.

The first formulation of the problem, however, is at least consistent with Marxist epistemology in that it allows subjectivity' or 'individuality' or 'personality' to be an effect of discoverable causes and does not regard the subject as a pre-found agent and source of its own production. Yet even on this interpretation it remains unclear what role Sartre would think a heuristically adequate Marxism should assign to biology. I therefore propose to give the challenge a more directly materialist formulation. The question then becomes: what account would Marxism give of the relationship between biological and social factors in constituting the person? Does it allow biology a role at all? If so, how does it, or should it, theorize that role?

Finally, and overarching the more specific issues, there is a general and philosophical challenge to the effect that Marxism, in its neglect of nature and biology, has compromised on the materialism of its thought. This has been expressed most forcefully and eloquently by the Italian Marxist, Sebastiano Timpanaro, who charges Marxism with idealism to the extent that it suppresses or ignores the 'infra-infrastructure' of the biological and argues himself that it is only in the recognition of the latter that one constitutes a truly materialist theory.[5] Timpanaro lays particular stress on certain 'infra-infrastructural' determinations – subjection to illness, old age and death – which he speaks of as 'givens' of the human condition. It is only, he argues, in our acceptance of such obstacles to human happiness that we endow Marxism with a hedonist-pessimist dimension that it lacks, or discovers, and then only partially, in the work of Engels.

It should be stressed that Timpanaro is no crass materialist: he is careful to distinguish his position from the reactionary naturalism or biologism of those who would account for

historical change and development in terms of geographica
factors, or explain class division and social conflict in purel
biological or ethnic terms; nor does he expose an ahistoric
essentialist account of biological determinations for he i
quite prepared to cede that biology is for the most par
'socially mediated' and that our biological constitution i
itself subject to evolution even if its 'history' proceeds at a
much slower pace than that of the history of society. But he
would argue that the determination of certain biologica
'givens' is prior to and overrides any social determination, and
that it is only if Marxism is prepared to recognize this fac
that its explanations of human history can count as trul
materialist.

Materialism and the Human Sciences

I shall here pursue some of the general epistemological issue
raised by this last 'challenge' since a discussion of them i
essential to establishing the position from which, I shal
argue, one must approach the relations between biology and
society and which I shall later exemplify in more detail.

In the first place, since Timpanaro does not confine hi
claim about the recognition of the 'infra-infrastructure' t
historical materialism alone, but argues (see, for example, hi
essay on 'Structuralism and its Successors'[6]) that the scienti
ficity or 'materialism' of the human sciences in genera
depends upon this recognition, he recalls us to the question o
the relationship between the systems studied by thes
sciences and their 'material' basis in organic or inorgani
matter. Are their studies only scientific to the extent tha
they are able to offer a physical explanation of the phenomen
they investigate, or should one accept that one may discove
these phenomena to be quite specific in kind so that, a
N. Chomsky has argued in regard to our linguistic capacity,
'physical explanation' will only be discovered in the un
interesting terminological sense that the term 'physical' wil
be extended to include whatever is discovered in their domai
'exactly as it was extended to accommodate gravitational an
electromagnetic force, massless particles, and numerous othe
entities and processes that would have offended against th
common sense of earlier generations?'[7]

That Timpanaro can find nothing but obscurantism and a triumph of spiritualism in this Chomskyan position suggests that for him there is no alternative: either one opts for an outright Cartesian separation between the mental and the physical and therefore denies any possible connection between the objects of the sciences concerned with mental phenomena and the sciences concerned with physical phenomena; or else one must recognize that the scientificity of studies at the non-physical level depends on their capacity to provide physicalistic explanations of their objects of study. The implication, that is to say, is that it is only the reducibility of the mental to the physical that will restrain one from the flight into spiritualism and the abandonment of science.

Now obviously a Cartesianism that posits a radical heterogeneity of mental and physical and thus allows, at least conceptually, for the absolute independence and autonomy of the mental is mistaken; but so too is the reductionist position to the extent that it abstracts from the specificity of the data studied by psychology and is too ready to confine its studies only to data than can be given an obviously natural and physical explanation. For it is arguable that this restriction imposes an arbitrary and unscientific principle of selection that belies the actual complexity and particularity of the data of which the theory should take account if it is to be anything like an adequate theory. That Chomsky has discovered our linguistic capacity to be hitherto intractable to physical explanation does not necessarily imply imply that he has proceeded unscientifically; it may, on the contrary, be the position to which he has been led by his preparedness to explore the full specificity of his object of study and by his refusal to be seduced into mistakenly analogic forms of explanation (such as are found in much comparative ethology) that in fact betray the real nature of the empirical data they investigate.

It is for reasons of this kind that I believe one must reject any hasty identification of a materialist epistemology with the recognition of the natural and biological 'infra-infrastructure'. By contrast, a materialist theory must recognize the full extent of the relative autonomy and specificity of the ideational and mental systems studied by the non-biological human sciences. For it is not the discovery as such of physical matter that guarantees their materialism but rather their correspondence with the reality they attempt to appropriate in thought. This does not mean that such systems can be conceptualized independently of their physical support; nor does it imply that a physical or neuro-physiological explanation of the processes and phenomena they study might not ultimately be discovered and go to confirm and complement their studies. But in the first place, a study of a system such as human language, or the unconscious, must pursue the full extent of the specificity of its object at the level at which it discovers it; and, in the second place, a neuro-physiological explanation of our linguistic capacity or of the processes studied by psychoanalysis would not destroy or render redundant the validity of studies which aim precisely at theorizing effects discoverable at a particular level, and in their particular systematicity at that level.

In other words, an anti-reductionist methodology will be justified even if ontological distinctions between the objects of the various natural and human sciences are discovered – as in fact both Marx and Freud respectively predicted or hoped would be the case – to be unnecessary. For even if, as Marx suggested, 'natural science will in time include the science of man as the science of man will include natural science', there is still the question of how one differentiates between the various levels of investigation that co-exist within this single science. Though it remains in principle feasible that eventually a system of correlations and connections between social and psychic and natural processes, will be discovered one can only begin the task of its discovery after a science has pursued the full extent of the autonomy of its social or psychic object and the search for a unified system should not be allowed prematurely to determine the course of any scientific study.

The implication of all this for historical materialism is that the 'materialist' character of its thought cannot simply lie in its acknowledgement that physical matter pre-exists all human thought and action and exerts its particular determinations upon the latter. For in itself that is no solution to the problem of what makes our relationship to that though and action a relationship of scientific (materialist) knowledge. Indeed the reassertion of the natural and biological dimension does not distinguish Marxist materialism either from naturalism and biologism as explanatory theories of society and of the individual or from certain empiricist and idealist epistemologies that are at odds with Marxism. This means that any Marxist materialist theory of the relations between the natural and social and psychological sciences must extend beyond a statement of the existential primacy of the physical and biological, for it is Marxist not simply by virtue of its recognition of the prior determination of the natural and biological 'infra-infrastructure' but by virtue of its capacity to provide knowledge at the level at which these general determinations make their appearance as specific and always 'socially mediated' effects within society.

I have already suggested that the identification of the materialism of historical materialism with its recognition of the 'infra-infrastructure' only exists as a tendency in Timpanaro's argument since he agrees on the 'socially mediated' concrete existence of biological 'givens' and would therefore presumably acknowledge that as such they provide the object for a particular enquiry. But I do believe that his zeal to assert the claims of the biological 'givens' to attention leads him to neglect or deny the importance of epistemological distinctions that need to be maintained if one is not to confound general determinations with their particular effects. General biological determinations are not to be contrasted with, or put in competition with the particular effects of historical social relations in the way that Timpanaro suggests they can be; and in contrast to the idea that any knowledge, except of the most general kind, can be given of human society simply in the statement of the co-existence of general biological determinations and particular social relations one must assert the importance of a study directed at the order of this co-existence itself: human culture is the effect of an interaction between biological and social determinations and it is crucial to an understanding of it that it is approached as the particular product of that interaction. Timpanaro tends to present the 'biological' and the 'social' as if they designated separate kinds of existence that 'mix' together while nonetheless retaining a pure, identifiable status within that mixture. In fact the effect produced by this conjunction is much more of the nature of a compound different in kind from either of its 'pure' ingredients, and it is knowledge of this 'compound' which is at stake in the study of human culture, and which forms the object of a specific kind of inquiry even if it will be one that makes use of sciences directed at a knowledge of the 'ingredients' taken in abstraction from each other.

Despite these epistemological differences, it should be clear from what I have said so far that I am not of a mind to dispute with Timpanaro the importance of biological determinations. I also think that he is right to pose the question of the extent to which Marxism either inherently or in its contemporary 'distortions' supports a false reduction of natural to social determinants. Indeed, I think he is correct to suggest that Marx himself provides a 'propitious terrain' for such a socialization of the natural because of a lack of clarity in certain of his formulations, though I do not believe that this lack of clarity is 'never completely overcome even in Marx's mature thought'.[8]

After all, the very insistence upon the primacy of the socio-economic order can easily incline one to underestimate natural determinations, and if pushed too far will lead to a denial that nature has any active role in the development of human culture at all – at least after a certain stage in its history. When that happens, nature comes to be viewed as a mere backdrop to a *deus ex machina* of social relations which really has all the action. The importance of Marx's work, one is told, lies in the fact that he sees nature as historical – as a nature that is constantly transformed by human action. That is true enough provided this transformative power is not interpreted in a way that reduces nature to a passive materiality, a sleeping partner, that is offered up to an omnipotent and self-activating praxis rather than itself acting as a continuing determinant upon the forms of its appropriation and mutation.

It seems to me that the kind of freedom and transcendence over nature that is ascribed to humanity on such a view, has not, despite its alleged Marxism, entirely escaped from the conception of the relations between man and nature that dominated seventeenth- and eighteenth-century political theory. The latter, as we know, opposed the 'Natural Individual', whose province was the 'State of Nature' to his social existence in 'Civil Society', and it viewed this 'Natural Individual' as always separated, even before 'entry into' society, from the naturality (that is bestiality) of the animal world at large by virtue of certain essentially human characteristics which the society he enters is designed to protect. Man is viewed as an already developed creature in the essential naturality of that individuality which separates him from the gregarious-sociality of the animal world at large, and his 'Civil Society' merely goes to confirm that status; it is not conceived as the vehicle itself of his development, his 'hominization'. Isolation from nature is the content itself of the essential human spirit.

Now, as it is also known, Marx was in fact the most damning critic of this liberal conception which is the target of his biting attack on the 'Robinsonade illusions' of seventeenth- and eighteenth-century political-theorists. He there exposes the 'Natural Individual' as none other than the developed bourgeois individual of their own contemporary society 'read back' into history as history's starting point and shows how the superficial individuality of the member of bourgeois society is confirmed in an ideological account of his origin and socialization that denies the continuity of the animal and human world, and endorses what is in fact a quite artificial separation of man from nature. In other words, humanity is always conceived as by definition opposed to naturality rather than as a specific form of its existence. In contrast to this view, Marx offers a different sense of naturality in accordance with which the developed bourgeois individual who is reflected in the mythical 'Natural Individual' is indeed natural in the sense that he is the product of that always social 'natural' order which is human culture, and the society in which he finds himself is that which has produced his very individuation and is the latest historical form of the 'natural' sociality-gregarious: it is indeed 'social' because it is 'natural' to be social. In short, man in naturally social, and his development as man – the process of 'hominization' – takes place in and through society.

In what sense, then, given that Marx completely inverts the

discourse of liberal theory, does one find allegedly Marxist accounts of the man–nature relationship that reproduce its underlying theme? Only in the sense that the emphasis on man's creativity, his self-activating 'praxis' tends to the denial that man is what he is because of an interaction with nature in which both the subjective element of human praxis and the objective determinations of nature are active. For in that event one is referred again to the view that man's essential nature, his 'species-being', lies in his control and transcendence over nature: nature is absorbed into human nature and the latter is thereby rendered immune to that animal and bestial nature which still dominates all other species and to which all save man must remain obedient. Of course, the analogy between this Marxism of 'praxis' and liberal thought is not perfect, since the former does not deny the sociality of man; nor does it distinguish man from animal by virtue of what are only the historical effects of his productive activity (his 'freedom', 'autonomy', possession of property etc.) but by virtue of that productive activity itself. But there is an analogy to the extent that if viewed in terms of a total control and undetermined creativity this productive capacity itself acquires a spiritual dimension: it is that which in the absorption even of nature into the human subject effectively separates all animal history from human history and contrives the latter's authentic destiny.

Such a conception is not only encouraged by certain of Marx's remarks taken in isolation; it is also the effect of a quite understandable desire to develop a Marxist theory of the man – nature relationship beyond what I shall argue is the limited form in which it is found explicitly stated in Marx's work itself. It is ambiguities and limitations in Marx's express statements that encourage distortions. For example, though Marx exposes the mystificatory character of the concepts of naturality and sociality that are found in liberal discourse, he does so more by way of collapsing sociality into naturality than by replacing them with concepts that mark a difference between the natural and the social within the order of human culture. It is implied in the critique of liberalism that neither the concept of naturality nor that of sociality can be used as a concept of man's difference from the animal world, both being rather concepts of his continuity with that world. Marx's appeal to the essential sociality of man is not an appeal to a difference but to a sameness; that is both its strength and also its limitation. For while in the liberal and pseudo-Marxist versions the terms natural and social are given a specifically human reference, with Marx this is not the case; the solution he offers is utterly general. It is for this reason that one needs to extend upon it – for if one is simply content with a statement to the effect that everything that is natural for man is also social, and everything that is social is also natural, one abstracts from any knowledge of humanity's specific naturality and sociality and is deprived of any criterion for assessing their respective roles in determining the order of human culture. Granted that the interpretation of the nature/society distinction of seventeenth- and eighteenth-century political theory is a piece of mystifying self-reflection, does this mean that there is no substantive difference that the terms should be used to retain and specify? Indeed, unless such a distinction is made, how can one ever differentiate the Marxist position from one or another form of reductionism?

I would argue in similar vein apropos that other dictum to which appeal is so often made in explication of Marx's views on this topic, namely, the sixth thesis in *Theses on Feuerbach*: 'The human essence is no abstraction inherent in each single individual. In its reality it is the ensemble of social relations'. Now of course, it has been said often enough that Thesis 6 is enigmatic, or it is only a germ or it is merely gestural – and, indeed, the midwives of this pregnant aphorism have contrived to bring to light some rather differing progeny[9] – but the fact of the matter is that one is inclined to forget one's own advice about its gestural and enigmatic quality and to regard it as a highly positive and final statement. In fact, I would argue, its import is largely negative, consisting as it does in the denial of essentialist accounts of human nature. Certainly this has positive implications, but these need to be carefully investigated. Otherwise one could be so blinded by the enlightenment that is introduced in the concept of the 'ensemble of social relations' that there is a risk of falling back within the structure and terms of discussion that the 'Thesis' in fact indicates one should move beyond. In other words, it is

very seductive to interpret the 'Thesis' as a simple reversal of
the relations of opposition and priority between natural and
social, so that instead of the individual and natural relations
being conceived as prior to and determinant upon society, it
is social relations that are accorded a primacy and total
determination over the natural. Viewed in this light, however,
the 'Thesis' becomes a justification for privileging social
relations in a way that betrays what is arguably Marx's essential insight on human culture, namely that it is a specific
union of man with nature in which neither the so-called social
nor the so-called natural features have primacy.

But then, if one recognizes this truth, and refuses to be
persuaded into the false, but superficially attractive 'conclusion' of the 'Thesis', one has to confront the fact that it
does not go much beyond that initial postulate of the sociality
of man; it is, after all, only a very general and preliminary
statement. If social relations are regarded, correctly, as the
very vehicle itself of man's interaction with the natural world,
rather than as a set of artificial accretions about his essentially
natural self, they can no longer do duty as the concept of the
difference between the 'natural' and 'social' factors that enter
into that interaction.

It is because the statements in which Marx explicitly
criticizes liberal discourse *are* so general and abstract that
one can only fully understand their import if one goes beyond
them to the point where their insight is fully realized, namely
in the analysis of *Capital*.

To put this another way, *if* Marx can be said to transcend
rather than reproduce, albeit in inverted form, the discourse
of an opposition between natural and social, it is because he
refuses once and for all to offer a 'philosophic' solution to the
question of the relations between natural and social determinations and therefore opens up this question to scientific
investigation. If one looks, for example, at the extreme care and
detail with which Marx in *Capital* studies the labour-process,
and reveals this to be a product of effects that divide between
the natural-technical on the one hand, and the social on the
other, one is bound to acknowledge that the approach is quite
at odds with any general dismissal of the problem in terms of
the 'socialization' of nature.

Of course, there *is* an abstract, theoretical solution implicit in *Capital*, which is that already mentioned, namely, that human society, which is itself a part of the natural world, must be analysed as a *unity* of natural and social factors; but though this unity is exemplified, its form is never explicitly theorized. Concepts are produced (those of the 'forces of production' and 'relations of production') that are pertinent to that distinction, but they are not the conceptualization of this distinction itself, and Marx does not expressly state what he regards to be the specific features of social production that are designated on the one hand 'forces' and on the other hand 'relations'. What he does do, however, in the very analysis of capitalist production, rather than in any general epistemological statement, is to exemplify the concepts; and it is through this exemplification itself that one becomes aware of the recalcitrance of real, material production to any 'appropriation in thought' that collapses the specific unity of natural and social effects into an identification of one with the other. He suggests, that is, that the precise character of this unity is discovered not by a purely philosophic or rational exercise, but through investigation of its particular presence in society.

Now if this is the case, what does it imply for an understanding of Marx's transcendence of the problematic of bourgeois thought? It implies, I think, that in place of the idea of a human culture divided between two ontologically separate realms of the 'natural' and the 'social' which can be dissolved into each other at the touch of a philosophic wand, there is the idea of a single, unified order that can be studied at different levels of abstraction because of distinct differences (which need to be specified) between the various determinants upon its formation, but which itself only exists as a particular combination of the effects of those determinations. It must, therefore, be known as that combination even if in order to arrive at this knowledge one needs to be able to think of it both in the 'one-sidedness' of its natural existence and in the 'one-sidedness' of the socio-economic relations that embody that natural existence. To return to the example of the labour-process[10]: in the first instance Marx discusses this as a purely natural process, its 'naturality' being specified in

terms of the organic and inorganic properties of the physical
elements and processes that take part in it. But this 'abstract'
account is subsequently corrected by elaboration of the social
relations, specified in terms of the extraction of surplus-value,
that enter into the determination of the capitalist labour-
process and give to it its particular content. The concept of
the labour-process thus becomes the concept of a multi-
determined object of a quite specific kind but whose natural
and social determinants remains nonetheless specifiable.

Biology and Society

It seems to me that Marx's treatment of the labour-process
presents a kind of exemplar for a materialist approach to
questions about the way in which one should think the forms
of unity between biological and social determinations that
are instantiated both socially and individually. This is an
approach which recognizes that human production takes
place as a result of an appropriation of nature by agents who
are biologically determined even if that nature is continually
transformed by their actions, and even if genetic determinations always manifest themselves as specific because
they are only present in particular historico-social contexts.
It is not that natural determinants gradually disappear and
become submerged in social determinants, but that these
natural determinants can never be explained wholly in terms
of physical and biological properties for they are always
materialized as particular cultural products. For example,
human beings are naturally determined in various ways by
virtue of a common biological structure: they are endowed
with certain somatic instincts, a certain physiognomy, a
certain level of physical strength, a certain sex and therefore a
certain role in reproduction and so on. But it is how these
instincts are satisfied, the value conferred on particular
physical attributes, the ways in which physical strength is
harnessed, the forms in which sexual division is lived and
experienced, that are central to any understanding of the
concrete effects of these determinations: it is these social
features that in a real and important sense render the natural
a cultural product. This, however, does not mean that their
explanation can be given wholly in terms of social relations.

It is therefore desirable, in order to avoid confusion, and to escape the circle of polemical dispute between a biologistic reduction on the one hand and a 'socialistic' reduction on the other, to introduce certain epistemological distinctions that will delineate more clearly between different objects of investigation and give a more precise definition to terms such as 'biological', 'social', 'biology', 'society', that have hitherto tended to remain ambiguous in status.

These distinctions are based on the premise that it is possible to distinguish between various different sciences each possessed of its own object. First, I propose to retain the term 'biology' to designate a science whose object is the structure and properties of living organisms and of their specific differences. This is a science which operates at a certain level of abstraction in that its concepts explain these structures and properties as they exist *generally* for different animal populations: it does not explain the particular differences to be found in particular animal or insect populations which are the effects of concrete determinations. Second, as a branch or sub-section of this science, there is the science of human biology, whose object is the specifically human organism conceptualized at the non-historical, physical level. It operates at a similar level of abstraction from the concrete differences between human societies and individuals and cannot therefore itself be used to explain certain historical and individual phenomena. On the other hand, a third area of investigation – which provides the object of what I propose to call 'social biology' – will be defined by reference to the object and concepts used in the science of human biology. The object of this social biology will be the effects of biological structures and properties as they are found at the level of specific 'societies'. That is to say, within the study of the social formation as a whole it is possible to distinguish sub-sections or levels of study one of which will provide the object of social biology; the level is defined in its case by the fact that the socialized concretizations that it studies are those which relate directly to the biological structures and properties (somatic instincts and their 'basic biological needs', sex difference, physical properties responsible for human forms of growth, senescence, illness and so on) which provide the object of human biology. At the same time, it is obviously impossible to delineate the terms of reference of this study in any very precise way, for the effects that it studies are multi-determined – they are points of convergence of a totality of determinants some of which are biological, but many of which will have to be specified as effects of economic, political and ideological practices – so that a study of these practices will always be involved in a study of social biology.

It might be objected at this point that since I am making these distinctions on the basis of an understanding of human culture as a unity of natural and social factors, I should therefore allow that *all* social relations bear the imprint even if very indirectly, of biological determinants; therefore this social biology is involved everywhere in the study of society and I have collapsed its specificity again into the generalized study of social relations. In reply to this, I would assert that there is a difference of degree that amounts to a difference in kind in the directness with which biological determinations enter into various social practices, and that social biology attains its relative autonomy precisely in its recognition of this difference. To put it crudely, they enter more directly into medical than into aesthetic practices, they are more central to kinship structures than to legal structures, and so on. Granted that it is allowed that the effects of biological determinations permeate everywhere and are coincident with the 'social' order, there still remains the task of distinguishing the specificity of the 'biological' at the level of social relations. I attempt to make this distinction by arguing for an area of relative autonomy that is provided on the one hand by a distinction between social biology and human biology, and on the other hand by its concentration upon those social relations and their experienced effects which pertain most directly to human biology.

Though I have exemplified this epistemological distinction only for biology, it can be generalized: any theory of society or of the individual remains gestural if it merely offers a resolution of these in the homogeneity of 'social relations'; for as it stands this formula gives no indication of the pertinences of the particular distinctions to be made between different dimensions or levels at which these relations exist and different practices which they embody. Furthermore,

I see no objection in principle to the constitution of some similar social object of investigation in relation to inorganic nature. This would have to do with the specific effects in particular economies and branches of those economies at particular times of the physico-chemical properties of inorganic matter – their impact upon forms of technology, the limits they impose upon material production, the extent of the 'elasticity' allowed to various human attempts to control and manipulate nature, and the short- and long-term effects of our neglect of natural determinants. Clearly this is a study with close affinities to ecology, though distinguished from much that passes for scientific investigation in that area by its concentration upon the role played by the mode of production in determining the ways in which natural determinants are experienced. Such a study would illuminate the concepts of 'productive forces' and 'relations of production', allow us to see their forms of autonomy and interdependence and thus to avoid simplistic accounts of these issues in terms either of the 'neutrality' of technology, on the one hand, or its total containment by social relations on the other.

There is one final epistemological distinction that I want to draw here because it relates so directly to the main topic of this paper. This regards the relations between human biology and psychology. I take the latter to be an autonomous domain of study concerned with mental as opposed to bodily processes and I have already suggested the extent to which I regard the object of the human sciences concerned with these processes (for example the study of language, perception, learning etc.) to be quite specific. I also believe that psychoanalysis has revealed a similar specificity in the structures and mechanisms which govern the transformation of somatic instincts – primarily sexual instincts – into psychic experiences, and has shown these to have a high degree of universality and permanence. But just as human biology studies its object in isolation from the socio-economic context, so too does a psychology that is concerned with fundamental and universal psychic properties; and even psychoanalysis, though it is concerned with mental activity as affected by, and in the context of, interpersonal and familial relations, tends to treat the latter as a kind of permanent, synchronic background to the diachrony of individual psychic responses, rather than

as themselves a fluctuating set of relations whose properties
change along with those of society at large. For example,
though it may be true that repression is almost as permament a
feature of our mental lives as is the need for food of our
somatic existence, the particular content of repressed material
will be subject to change – and not simply as a result of the
contingencies of an individual confrontation with others
(in particular the others of the family) but as an effect of the
movement and pattern of change of society as a whole. One
can therefore conceive of a study complementary to that of
social biology whose object would be the specific social content of the effects of psychic determinants. Social biology will
constantly make use of the results of this 'social psychology'
and in a sense will contain it, because these psychic determinants in their specific concretizations will themselves be
among the determinants of which a social biology will need
to take account in its understanding of how biological determinations are instantiated at any point and subjectively
experienced.

Of course, it might be objected that my argument licences a
proliferation of 'scientific objects' that must eventually
undermine the notion of what constitutes a science. It would
not particularly bother me if it were thought necessary to
retain the term 'science' only for studies at a higher level of
abstraction than those engaged in by 'social biology', 'social
psychology' etc. for I am fully prepared to acknowledge the
extent to which the objects of investigation of the latter differ
from those of the sciences proper both in the less abstract
level at which they are found and in the fuzziness of their
borderlines, the degree to which they overlap each other.
All that I would insist upon is the relative autonomy of these
areas of investigation and the importance of studies cast at
their level to any knowledge of society or the individual.

I propose now to substantiate and exemplify this claim by
way of discussion of the specific issues raised by those
'challenges' to which I referred above.

The forms of existence of biology in society

Sex Difference
Feminists have poured scorn on Freud's claim that 'anatomy

is destiny'; but they have been equally dismissive of any Marxist attempt to reduce sexual relations to economic and class relations. On the one hand, there is a rejection of the idea that sexual oppression is biologically determined; on the other hand, there is a rejection of the idea that it is wholly the effect of socio-economic determinants. Both rejections have their particular truth: the point is to extract and synthesize these truths, for otherwise one is bound to oscillate between two equally false positions each of which leads to voluntarist forms of politics. In the one case, one simply denies that human biological determinations have or need have any effect – a view embodied in a deliberate and ascetic political programme of resistance to biological impulses (typically involving the refusal to consort with or raise children with the male sex, the construction of exclusively female communities and so on). This is a programme that is ambiguous between a *refusal* to be woman biologically and an attempt to render her *biologically independent* of the male, and it is elitist in two related ways: it isolates female problems from those of human society and its humanity as a whole, and it is divisive between women themselves, since it constructs a moralism as to what constitutes female emancipation and then invites the majority of women, who are no less victims of sexual oppression and in many cases explicit opponents of it, to feel guilty of a betrayal of their sex to the extent that they cannot espouse or feel happy in this form of emancipation. The alternative position leads to a similar politics but via a somewhat different route: it rightly sees that sexual oppression cannot be explained wholly in terms of economic determinants, but in stressing this it comes to accord sexual determinants a priority over social ones which means that the former become the prime principle of historical explanation. This again separates the problem of female emancipation from that of the emancipation of society as a whole, and encourages the view that the former can be accomplished within the existing economic structure (through wages for housework and the like); it also means that faced with the apparent eternalization of sexual relations that would be a right-wing 'deduction' from the biologistic premises of this position, a left-feminist politics is forced again into 'revolutionizing' biology itself (through denial of female biological roles etc.): if things are ever going to change then it is biology itself that must be transformed or sublimated.

It is only if one recognizes that 'anatomy' *is* 'destiny' in the sense that biological sex difference does and will always have its effects upon human society that one can avoid these forms of impasse. It is impossible to escape from the biological roles of male and female in reproduction, and from the fact that the child is highly dependent for a very long period on adult care, and from certain physical and psychological differences between men and women in the experience of their own sexuality, and even perhaps from all manifestations of aggression, possessiveness, jealousy etc. But what can and must be changed is the particular containment of these biological effects in patriarchal society. Even the so-called 'biological' family is a cultural, not a natural product, and while a woman must necessarily bear and give birth to her child, it is by no means necessary for her to be wholly or largely responsible for its nurture. The argument could be elaborated in detail to show how it is particular and historically determined systems and institutions that converge in their determinations upon a given biological fact such as sex difference in order to give it the presence that it has socially and individually. This presence is in a profound sense the content itself of sex difference since it is its only actual embodiment in society; the point is to understand, on the basis of study at the level of social biology, to what extent this content is socially produced and therefore in principle transformable, to what extent it is naturally determined in ways that will continue to apply and of which account must be taken in any attempt to transform it.

Freud's dictum is a condemnation only if it is interpreted biologistically to mean that the role of woman in society is and always will be predetermined by the fact of her sexuality in the ways that it currently is; but if the 'destiny' is understood as the recognition of the role played by social relations in determining the ways in which biological difference becomes cultural difference, then it is clear that the 'destiny' of female subordination can be replaced by the 'destiny' of equality given radical changes in the social base. But such changes would not mean that either women or men would cease to have a destiny attributable precisely to the biological sex difference; in regard to *this* destiny, rather than bemoan some inquality it supposedly betokens, one should recognize that here the concept of equality is quite inappropriate since one is concerned with a destiny that cannot be shared; and perhaps one should rejoice in that fact. It is, I suggest, for social not for biological reasons that the celebrants of 'Vive la différence!' happen today to be mainly male and chauvinist.

On needs

It is sometimes said that what is distinctive about Marx's approach to the question of human needs is that he recognised their 'historically developed' character; but in fact, no theorization about needs has been so naïve as wholly to deny that fact, so that when Marx asserts, in opposition to bourgeois economic theory, the priority of production over consumption and the historical nature of needs, his attack is more directed at the implications of the bourgeois standpoint if taken to its logical conclusion than against any conception of needs it explicitly espouses. In other words, Marx goes some way in his arguments to expose the muddleheadedness of any economic account that views production as simply designed to meet the needs of consumption for that account obviously leads to insuperable problems when it comes to the explanation of the actual development of needs – either one recognises the expansion of needs but cannot explain it, or else one must assume that all the needs of contemporary man are found present in his ancestors. But though Marx exposes the confusion in that account and the way it tends to essentialize the developed needs of bourgeois society, it is not as if he himself either in his arguments for the dominance of production or in the appeal to the historical nature of needs presents us with any real theory of the latter: conceptual distinctions between different kinds of needs and between their sources of production are extremely embryonic. Even if it is argued that Marx's conception of their historic character is quite distinctive, and lies in the fact that he conceived needs not merely as developed forms of an essential content but as specific historical contents (so that he does not think in terms of an essential human nature possessed of a given set of needs that are simply altered in the form of their satisfaction, but in terms of a human nature that itself changes in its structure of needs) one might still want to object that there are some needs (for example biological needs) that are more 'basic', universal and permanent than others, and which would have to be distinguished from less basic or purely historically produced needs. Now I would argue that it is precisely these kinds of distinctions—implicit in much talk, including that of Marx, about needs—which must be conceptualized by any 'theory of needs' worthy of that name, and which one can at least begin to provide on the basis of the epistemological distinction between natural and biological determinations and their socially mediated existence.

It would be a mistake, however, to think that such distinctions are only important in an academic sense since the development of a theory of needs has a crucial political role to play in the struggle for socialism and in its construction. Any successful politics of control and reorganization of the structure of consumption will need to be based on a realistic appraisal of the way in which natural and biological determinants enter into our lives in specific fashion at specific times. Even if a socialist economy were relatively free of external economic constraints,[11] its planning would still need to take account of the ways in which the properties of inorganic matter determine the appropriateness of particular technologies, levels of growth and modes of consumption. It will also need to plan with an eye to what are in fact currently felt to be needs by the members of society. It would be as politically naïve of socialism to attempt to transform an inherited pattern of consumption overnight as it is politically irresponsible in the world today to propagandize about 'unlimited expansion of material needs', 'constant development of the productive forces' and suchlike. It is naïve in the one case because it abstracts from the effects of biological and psychological determinations and thus tends to suggest that human beings are transformed in their habits as an automatic result of economic changes; and it is irresponsible in the other because it fails to take account of ecological constraints and plays upon an illusory concept of 'technical progress' which it has adopted wholesale from capitalism.

The errors of both these positions are ultimately accountable to a failure to take sufficient account of the complexity
of the interaction between socio-economic, biological and
natural factors that renders both production and affective
response to that production what they are at any given
historical point in time.

Obviously, not all historically developed needs are structured directly upon 'basic' somatic needs, but what I have
termed a 'social biology' can help us to understand the
development of those that are, to specify their contemporary
content and to think about the limits within which one
expects to be able to transform that content. It can also enable
us to differentiate conceptually between degrees to which
needs bear the imprint of biological determinations – between
needs that Marx, for example, characterized as historically
developed 'natural' needs, such as those for food, shelter,
sexual relations etc., and 'wholly historic' needs, such as that
for money, even though we recognize the latter to be affected
by psychological determinations (that enter into the 'auri
sacra fames', the 'magical significance' of money and its
'secret relations' with the individual), and even if it ultimately
makes sense only because of the access it provides to the
satisfaction of other needs.

It is only if one is prepared to recognize that consumption
is determined both directly by economic determinations
and indirectly by anthropological factors that one can
challenge the assumption common to both economistic and
naturalistic accounts of needs, namely, that there is automatic
correspondence between production and consumption. An
essential human nature no more determines a social production than a social production essentializes a specific human
nature. Neither the economistic account, which would
identify needs with 'effective demand', nor the naturalist
account, which seeks to explain supply on the basis of
demand, can logically allow that there can be contradictions
within a structure of needs, and they will therefore have to
obscure or deny the political implications of those contradictions.

The alternative is to recognize the extremely hetero-
geneous nature of the needs to which capitalist production
gives rise, and the various degrees in which it both satisfies

and frustrates. It is to recognize, that is, that one cannot abstract from the complexity and uneven development of the relations between production and consumption. Though it is correct to emphasize the dominance of production in determining needs as a corrective to any naturalization of consumption, it should also be kept in mind that production itself always reflects the moulding of an established pattern of consumption. It is because this interaction between needs and products is complex and bilateral, and bears the mark of many determinations other than those stemming directly from economic production and its particular distribution relations, that consumption is both specific to any stage of social development and contradictory in that specificity. The vitality of a socialist politics depends on the extent to which it can distinguish between the unnecessary contradiction inherent to a social production that determines use-value on the basis of exchange-value, and the necessary contradiction inherent to any society that attempts to *plan* to meet needs. Neither contradiction should be seen as an opposition between a brute nature and the manipulations of production; but the one is the malign effect of the dominance of the economic laws of capital accumulation, and the other is the benign index of the dominance of political decision; the latter is not contradiction to be resolved but rather to be lived.

The theory of the individual

There is a certain amount of confusion caused on this topic simply by virtue of the fact that a *theory* of the individual is not sufficiently distinguished from a knowledge of any concrete individual; strictly speaking, all that a theory can provide is the conceptual framework for thinking the more general and essential determinations that enter into the formation of *any* individual and which will combine in specific forms in the making of any particular person; it will conceptualize forms of individuality pertaining to differing kinds of determination (those of biology, class, family, education etc.) and which are common to many individuals; it can then go on to point to the way in which the specificity of the person is more nearly approached the more nearly one is able, and prepared, to chart the particular combination of such forms of individuality that apply in his or her case. But not only is there always a gap between this theoretical statement and its concepts and any actual living person; it is also the case that any particular individual will be the 'product' not only of the more essential determinations – which by virtue of their relative generality can provide the object of theory – but also of many accidental factors that could only be ascertained empirically. For that reason, the overall statement of any 'theory' of the individual would have to be to the effect that the person is the outcome of many determinations, some of them attributable to forms of individuality that can be specified in any particular case, and some of them fortuitous.

There are further confusions introduced because of fundamental differences in the way in which individuality is conceived. For so-called biologistic theories individuality is attributable basically to only one kind of determinant – that of biology: it is one's biological constitution, and ultimately that alone, which determines who one is. It appears in its crassest form in the work of pscyhologists such as Sheldon[12] who associates personality directly with a biological 'morphic' type. Very few, and least of all Marxists, have been prepared to grant much credence to such biological reductionism.

It would be a mistake, however, to suggest that biologism has only been attacked from the standpoint of a Marxist conception of the person, and for this reason it is important to distinguish this attack from various idealist views. For example, Marxism does not deny biologism in order to identify the individual at the level of the 'ego' or conscious subjectivity: Marxism has never conceived the person simply in terms of this conscious 'sense of self', or wholly at the level of conscious experience, since it has always seen the need to explain the production of that 'sense' and that 'experience' itself (and by and large, as one knows, it has wanted to give an account in terms of the social relations into which individuals enter unknowingly and independently of their wills). Nor is Marxism's rejection of biologism consistent with the existentialist conception of the subject in terms of a transcendent consciousness through whose 'projects' the personality, and even in a sense the biological self,[13] is 'chosen' and retrospectively constituted. Existentialism and Marxism may share a disdain for biological explanations of the person but in the case of Marxism it is not in order to maintain the wholly undetermined nature of the individual but rather to assert the claims to attention of determinations that are other than biological in nature.

In what, then, does, or should, a Marxist (that is a materialist but non-biologistic) theory of the individual consist? Now it seems to me that in offering us the concept of 'social relations' from which to approach the theorization of the individual Marxism makes a distinct advance upon the triad of positions outlined above (that is those of biologism, an empiricist identification of individual with conscious self, and existentialism). But there is always the risk in stressing the role of socio-economic determinations that biological determinations come to be regarded as nugatory and always subordinate in their effects upon personality, and this I shall argue is mistaken. Equally, there is the danger that the particularity of the person is dissolved and nullified in the general category of social relations. These two errors can compound each other, for if the denial of the role of biological determinations in the formation of the individual is combined with a failure to identify differences at the level of social relations, then there is no principle of individuation left at all.

I think Marxism has been very prone to this kind of dissolution of the subject and that it has never taken sufficient pains to distinguish claims to the effect that the 'individual is the product of social relations' from crude environmentalist and behaviorist theories of the person. Even L. Sève's account of personality, despite the excellence of its critique of bourgeois psychology and sociology, tends in that direction at least to the extent that he denies that a person's biological constitution has any role to play in individuation. Sève recognizes, of course, that individuals exist as biological and psychological subjects, but he would deny that a biological or psychic inheritance has any determination upon personality: for him the sole principle of explanation of personality is social relations, and even the biological organism must be theorized as a product of personality. Now Sève is absolutely right in his insistence upon the predominant role of determinations that are external to the person rather than the product of an internal inheritance in shaping personality, and he is clearly right in his concern to recognize that natural determinations never enter directly into its formation but are only found in the content that social relations have given to them. But in stressing their socially mediated aspect he tends to suppress their natural origin altogether and this means that a necessary difference between socially mediated *biological* determinations and determinations of a different order (those of class, family, education and so on) is collapsed in the single undifferentiated principle of explanation that he finds in social relations.

In contrast to this position it must be accepted that one's biological constitution does indeed have a role to play in determining one's personality even if the explanation of this role can never be given wholly in terms of human biology since how we live and experience our bodies, and the kind of importance they have for us, is at least as much accountable to social as to natural factors. It would, for example, seem to matter very much what sex or skin colour or physical appearance or degree of health one is endowed with, and these are all genetically determined. On the other hand, much of their significance is derived from the particular structure of production and the value-systems which sustain it, into which we are born. For that reason, there may be a considerable degree of difference in the extent to which the effects of biological determinations are dominant or subordinate in their 'importance' for the person relative to the effects of other social or less directly biological determinations. For example, one might want to suggest that they would be relatively dominant for most women and black persons today in many social contexts; or again, the less one approximates in terms of physical appearance to what is considered normal or attractive in the particular society in which one happens to be placed, the more significant this genetic determination is likely to be in the formation of personality; and similarly for those suffering from physical illness and handicaps of various forms. As I have tried to stress, the explanation of this dominance or subordination cannot be given in human biology: it is precisely because it cannot be explained in those

terms but still nevertheless involves them that social biology
is necessary to an understanding of the individual. That is to
say, any theory of the individual must include, and even begin
with, an account of the forms of individuality in which
biological properties which are common to many will be
specifically experienced by different groups at different times
in different social formations. Of course, even these forms of
individuality will be shared by many individuals, so that, as
suggested above, in order to approach more nearly to the
particularity of the person one will need to conceptualize
many additional forms of individuality pertaining to non-
biological aspects of existence. I have chosen to stress the
biological aspect here as a corrective to any Marxist tendency to 'reduce' the person wholly to social relations and
thus to 'socialize' what must be kept distinct as natural
determinants; but I hope I have done so in a way that would
distinguish my approach from the kind of reductionism that
is found in biologism.

Marxism and Materialism
Finally, as a way of drawing together these themes, I shall try
to summarize the main differences in my approach to the
biology–society relationship from that of Timpanaro, and to
exemplify them by reference to his claims about our biological
frailty.

Taken in its broadest sense I would agree with Timpanaro's
assertion of the role of natural and biological determinations.
Much of my argument has in fact been designed to show the
errors of attempts to deny their continuing effects; but I have
also been concerned to show that these effects never exist
concretely in a pure natural or biological form but only in the
content given them by socio-economic relations. One can
certainly study them in abstraction from those relations, and
this is the pursuit of the natural and biological sciences, but
where the object of our investigation is society itself one needs
to specify their social content, and a knowledge of society will
only be materialist if it is able to do so.

In contrast to the epistemological distinctions upon which
my position is based, and which invite us to conceive of
society not as a co-existence of two different and separate

ontological realms of the 'biological' and the 'social' but as a single unity of natural and social factors which can be studied at different levels of abstraction, Timpanaro asks us to conceive of the 'biological' as an ontological category, and tends to identify materialism with the recognition of this ontological realm. This means that ontological facts (biological structures and properties) are in themselves accorded an epistemological status and that their explanatory value is contrasted with, and somehow in competition with historical materialist explanation. Timpanaro stresses, quite rightly, that mankind is naturally and biologically determined, but he appears to think that a materialist explanation of human history is contained in this simple recognition of these general determinations abstracted from their particular effects. In this respect his account remains Feuerbachian – it presents us with an abstract generality, whereas Marxist materialism is distinguished by its recognition of the historical, and therefore always particular, existence of the entities and relationships that it studies. Its ontological materialism is therefore integrated with an epistemology based on this recognition. This means that its process of conceptualization, which will develop and organize concepts at various levels of abstraction, is deployed not in order to dissolve the particularities of specific instantiations into what they share in common, but as a system of reference points, a kind of scaffolding, for the construction of the particular object.

It should be emphasized that I am not charging Timpanaro with operating at a level of abstraction that fails to give us knowledge of the particular concrete effects of biological determinants in particular cases – even social biology remains abstract relative to the provision of that information – but with a failure to introduce conceptual distinctions necessary to a theorization of those effects. One must, for example, be able to differentiate between the biological instinct of hunger regarded as an attribute that holds universally, and *this* hunger for *this* kind of food, consumed in *this* kind of way; the latter can only be explained as a materialization of particular historical relations; it is not a mere *form* of abstract hunger and cannot therefore be conceptualized in the same terms.

Of course, Timpanaro does concede that biology itself is historicized and socialized; yet he appears to regard this historicization and socialization as *sui generis* – it has its particular pace and rhythm of change and this is a different pace and rhythm from that of the transformation of society. It is one thing, however, to recognize that the object studied by human biology is itself evolving, albeit very slowly, and therefore has its own 'history' (a history that without doubt will involve reference to social determinations just as does the history of any insect or animal evolution involve reference to environment); and it is another to recognize and chart the history of the social effectivity of the biological determinants whose changes are the subject of a history of biological evolution. The former, unlike the latter, does not take place in its own time but in the time of human society.

In any case, Timpanaro's main point is polemical. He wants to argue – and he does so for example specifically against L. Sève[14] – that even if the biological has in many respects become the social, this is not true in the case of those aspects of our biological nature (subjection to death, illness, old age) which comprise our 'biological frailty'. Thus to Sève, who claims:

> *The natural point of departure*, in the life of individuals as in that of social formations, is something quite other than the *real base of the developed totality*, the formation of the totality consisting precisely in the reversal of the relations between the natural and the social, in the progressive transformation of natural givens into historic results: within the developed individual even the organism has become to a large extent the *product* of the personality, in the historical materialist sense of the concept[15]

Timpanaro replies:

> This statement is generally correct, provided one bears in mind that such a generalization does not extend to certain givens of the human condition which are *still* very important and whose disappearance is still not foreseeable . . . The 'reversal' which Sève talks about is only a partial one, therefore, and it has taken place to a quite unequal degree in the various fields of human life and activity[16]

True enough – except that the givens of which *he* speaks

are never given as such, and in suggesting that they are, Timpanaro conflates the effects of biological determinations with those determinations themselves. Marx's insight on the necessity of grasping the historically developed content even of so-called 'basic biological needs' has no less relevance in regard to illness, death and old age than it has in regard to our need for food: 'Hunger is hunger, but the hunger gratified with cooked meat eaten with a knife and fork is a different hunger from that which bolts down raw meat with the aid of hand and nail and tooth'[17]

Illness is illness, death is death, but they have a specific content or 'significance' and they are experienced variously at different historical times by different social groups and classes and by individuals within those groups and classes. One has only to dwell for a moment on the history of the revelance of different diseases or on the extent to which they have differed through time in the menace they presented to human survival to realize the impossibility of any purely biological explanation of the specific manifestations of illness. Certainly it is genetically determined whether or not a person will suffer from haemophilia or brittle bones or diabetes but when and where that person is born will exert a good deal of determination on the effects of that determination. Or again, that a person suffers from illnesses of malnutrition, from bronchitis, from coronary thrombosis or from one or another form of mental illness is in almost all cases only partially to be attributed to biological determinations. Even death, that notorious leveller, will not lie down in the flatness of its essence, for though it comes to all, it comes in a thousand different ways, and its advent is regretted and welcomed and mythologized and celebrated not in the annals of biology but in those of society.

Still, it might be said: this is not the point. The point is that by virtue of our biological constitution we shall always be subject to illness in some form or another, to physical decay and to death. What is wrong with saying that we are biologically determined in this very general sense? The answer to this, I think, is that if one fails to make the kind of distinctions I have indicated it is all too easy to say of human society at any point: 'that is the human condition', and thereby to naturalize it, to collapse the difference between natural and social determinants operating within the social order and thus to relate to the latter as a form of the given. The human race is biologically determined in the sense that it has the kind of lungs which will be destroyed by over-exposure to a certain form of asbestos; and it is naturally determined in that asbestos has the physical and chemical properties that it does; but the incidence of asbestosis is a socially determined fact that it is within human capacities to alter. These determinations should be kept distinct.

I also think that there are certain silences in Timpanaro's account of the matter that must be seen as symptomatic by anyone endorsing my line of criticism. For example, it seems significant that sexuality – a hedonist-pessimist theme if ever there were one – scarcely features in his account of the biological infra-infrastructure. I suggest that this is because had he treated sexual division as an instance, along with death, old age and illness, of a continuing and inevitable biological feature of the human condition it would have appeared immediately obvious that certain conceptual distinctions would have to be introduced in order to avoid any reactionary endorsement of patriarchal relations; on the other hand, had he allowed for those distinctions then he would have had to realize that they had the same force in regard to those other biological features upon which he chooses to concentrate.

I believe the same considerations would come into play in any approach to psychology that similarly conflated effects with their determinations. For then one is inclined to eternalize certain attitudes or affective modes as inevitable human psychological givens. Thereupon it becomes all too clear how close one comes to a doctrine of innate dispositions characterizing 'human nature', thereby depriving oneself of all but voluntaristic arguments against the retrograde political positions 'deduced' from such doctrines.

The account of the 'natural' and 'biological' for which I have argued could be summed up as a substitution of epistemological distinctions for generalized ontological categories. No doubt in important respects it is closer to Sève's position than to Timpanaro's. But it parts company with Sève in the stress it lays upon the presence of certain effects attributable to biology and which render it important to constitute a specific domain of social biology. Sève's inclination is to dissolve all facts of existence into an undifferentiable soup of social relations, and to assimilate the latter to work relations. I think he is right to insist upon the importance of the 'reversal' of natural and social orders, which, in fact, I do not consider need be interpreted as a denial that certain general characteristics that can be designated biological are instantiated in society and impose their determinations upon its organization and activities. Where he goes wrong is in insisting that the *only* principle of the precise nature of these instantiations is contained in social relations, since it seems to be that human biology must be implicated in any explanation of those social relations themselves, and that it will enter very directly into a materialist account of certain human practices and experiences.

Notes

1   The quotation comes from Aristotle's *Politics*, I. 2, 9, where the sense of 'politikon' is 'living in a community', but its standard meaning is 'civic' or 'political'. Marx quotes it in the *Grundrisse* (Harmondsworth 1973), p. 84.

2   This has been a theme of much recent writing by French and Italian Marxists subsequent to the events in France of May 1968. See, for example, articles by A. Gorz in *The Division of Labour*, A. Gorz (ed.) (Hassocks 1976), and by M. Salvati and B. Beccalli, C. Donolo, and F. Ciafaloni in *Quaderni Piacentini* nos. 40, 41. See also *New Left Review*, no. 52. Very relevant to the theme is Hans-Magnus Ensensberger's article on the 'Critique of Political Ecology' in *New Left Review*, no. 84. Ensenberger writes that the ecologists, for all their blindness and naivete 'have one advantage over the utopian thinking of the Left in the west, namely the realization that any possible future belongs to the realm of necessity not that of freedom and that every political theory and practice – including that of socialists – is confronted not with the problem of abundance, but with that of survival'.

3   The 'problem', that is its fallacy, is discussed by L. Althusser, *Reading Capital* (London 1970), pp. 110–12.

4   See J.-P. Sartre, *The Problem of Method* (London 1963), pp. 53–7.

5   S. Timpanaro, *On Materialism* (London 1975).

6   S. Timpanaro, *op. cit.*, p. 135f.

7   N. Chomsky, *Language and Mind* (New York 1968), p. 84.

8   S. Timpanaro, *op. cit.* p. 40.

9   Of particular interest is the dispute between L. Sève and L. Althusser on the 'reading' of the 'Thesis' (see L. Althusser, *For Marx* (Harmondsworth 1969), pp. 242–8, and L. Sève, *Man in Marxist Theory and the Psychology of Personality* (Hassocks 1978), p. 161f. The main issue between them concerns the 'reality' of the human essence of which the 'Thesis' speaks. Whereas Althusser would reject the concretization of human essence on the basis that this involves an empiricist identification of thought object with real object, and leads straight to an explication of social relations in terms of interpersonal relations, Sève argues that essence has real existence, not only in particular objects but as itself a particular alongside all other objects, and he cites Marx's remarks in the *Grundrisse* on money ('the generality of all particular commodities' yet itself a particular alongside other commodities) and on abstract labour ('not only the category labour, but labour *in reality*, has here become the means of creating wealth in general . . . ') in support of the notion of concrete

essence. But is there not a considerable difference between pointing to the existence of a generality of social relations that is the product of *a particular stage of development of social relations*, and is embodied in money and the non-particularity of labour, and arguing for a human essence, which though always identified with the specific set of social relations, is nonetheless an always present essence, the automatic product of the social relations that define it? When Sève argues that one should understand the 'human essence' as an historical and concrete essence, that is as the instantiation in reality of a specific set of social relations, he confuses epistemological and ontological categories in such a way as to give us again a dumb generality in which all individuals participate, only this time the individuals are a specific set of historical individuals. The human essence is no more always the essence of its particular time than it is the essence of all time. The concept of essence of Thesis 6 can only be understood as a category of thought with which to grasp the general truth of the non-instantiation of essence in the real, just as the concept of 'production in general' remains a thought category, an abstraction, whose rationality lies in the fact that it brings attention to the factors common to all production *as factors* which are never concretized as such in any mode of production. The enigmatic quality of Thesis 6 derives from the ambiguity of the term 'reality' which can be read both as meaning 'has concrete existence' and as meaning 'only exists as a concept', that is as the general, abstract concept of the 'ensemble of social relations'.

10   K. Marx, *Capital*, I, chaps. 8 and 13–16.
11   Obviously I am abstracting here from all the constraints placed upon the development of socialist economies by virtue of the global economic context – at the present time predominantly capitalist – in which they are placed.
12   See, for example, W. H. Sheldon, *The Varieties of Temperament* (New York 1942).
13   Thus Sartre argues in *Being and Nothingness* (London 1958) that we choose even our birth in the sense that it is we alone who decide the bearing that the past is to have on us. See p. 490f.
14   S. Timpanaro, *op. cit.*, p. 215f.
15   L. Sève, *Men in Marxist Theory*, p. 213.
16   S. Timpanaro, *op. cit.*, p. 215.
17   K. Marx, *Grundrisse*, p. 92.

4 Natural Science and Cultural Struggle: Engels on Philosophy and the Natural Sciences

TED BENTON

Introduction : A Framework for Analysis

IT is the thesis of this paper that both modern philosophy and modern socialism have a great deal to learn from the re-reading and re-evaluation of the later writings of Engels on philosophy and the natural sciences. The texts with which I shall be most concerned are *Anti-Dühring*, *Dialectics of Nature*, *Ludwig Feuerbach and the End of Classical German philosophy*, as well as some items from the Marx-Engels correspondence. My argument will be that these texts were, amongst other things, the vehicle of Engels' contribution to contemporary popular debates on a range of topics from evolutionary theory to spiritualism, and that this must be the starting point for any modern re-evaluation of Engels' work. There are lessons, both positive and negative, for modern socialists, in Engels' way of dealing with these issues – especially where they concern the popular reception and application of new scientific knowledge. There are lessons, again both positive and negative, for modern philosophers in Engels' advocacy of a form of philosophical system-building which is now – unjustifiably, in my view – almost universally discredited among philosophers.

It is an assumption of this paper that the great majority of the modern opponents as well as proponents of dialectical materialist philosophy, whether they enter the debate principally as socialists or principally as philosophers, accept an interpretation of Engels' later work which is radically defective. Neither those who hold Engels and his dialectical materialist followers responsible for the 'naturalistic' and 'economistic' turn of the Second International,[1] nor those Marxists and non-Marxists alike for whom Engels is written off (or, still worse, defended!) as a pre-critical metaphysician who saw contradiction, negation and the play of the dialectic in every corner of the universe[2], – none of these modern 'authorities', has posed the question of Engels' intellectual project in its political and cultural setting. Nor have they penetrated the verbal appropriations of Hegel, to explore the real conceptual connections which provide the underlying unity of Engels' writings on philosophy and the natural sciences.

The purpose of my challenge to this widespread reading of Engels as participant in some timeless philosophical argument as to the ultimate nature and constitution of the universe, the relation between freedom and necessity, and so on, should not be misunderstood. I do not wish, nor do I think it possible to reveal 'the true', misunderstood, but ultimately victorious Engels, rescued from generations of misinterpretations. Even in the light of the re-evaluation I propose, Engels is committed to much that is both politically and philosophically objectionable. Rather, my point is that read as he usually is, without serious references to context, and as though Hegel were the substance, rather than the verbal form of his philosophical work, Engels lacks any real philosophical interest. His errors are, or would appear to be, fundamental, disastrous, elementary, and obvious. In short, what is inadequate about the 'orthodox' interpretation of Engels is, leaving aside its questionable scholarship, that it allows nothing constructive to come from the philosophical encounter with Engels.[3] Engels purported to provide answers to questions which should never have even been posed. That is all.

There have, of course, been writers – most notably Gareth Stedman Jones,[4] in this country, and Sebastiano Timpanaro, in Italy, who have not fallen victim to this orthodoxy, and who have written provocatively and with insight on Engels. My own work owes much to their efforts, and is an attempt to extend their investigations in a particular direction. My approach to the re-evaluation of Engels' work shares with Timpanaro' recognition of the need to understand his writings on the natural sciences as an intervention within a specific intellectual-political conjuncture. Only by characterizing that conjuncture, the encounters and alliances which characterized t, and the intellectual resources it made available, is it possible to pose on an adequate basis the question of the *objectives* of Engels' intervention, and the pertinence of the philosophical means of that intervention – the materialist inversion of Hegel's dialectic. Was Engels' whole intellectual project in his writings on the natural sciences constituted and determined by this appropriation of Hegel, or was the recourse to Hegel necessitated by intellectual-political problems definable and re-constitutable independently of the concepts of dialectical materialism, yet not soluble by means of any other philosophical instruments available to Engels? If the latter is the case, can Engels' intellectual project and his philosophical achievement be reconstituted without recourse to the defective philosophical instruments which yielded the dialectic of Nature? If, indeed, this can be done, is it an exercise which has relevance to our own situation? Are there continuities and partial parallels between the conjuncture of contemporary socialists and that of Engels which give his work a relevance to the current situation?

This much my approach to Engels' work on the natural sciences shares with Timpanaro. I am also indebted to his work for a number of important insights, but in important respects I part company with him. For Timpanaro, the central problem is, having recognized the dangers inherent in the 'speculative heritage' of dialectics, to 'single out all those things which were justifiably defended by the founders of Marxism and by their followers in the name of the dialectic – so that they can be formulated in a scientific manner'. The project of a 'scientific reformulation' of dialectical materialism is connected with Timpanaro's characterization of the *Dialectics of Nature* as calling for a 'logic of the historical sciences – a call that had become urgent ever since political economy (thanks to Marx) and the natural sciences (thanks to Lyell and Darwin) had incorporated the historical dimension'.[6]

Certainly the concern with historicity in nature and in human society is central to the *Dialectics of Nature* and Engels' other writings on the natural sciences, but the elaboration of a logic and methodology of the historical sciences is a specifically philosophical task. A recognition of the inadequacy of dialectics, as Engels employs them, to this task does not abolish the philosophical character of the task, or make it one reformulable in scientific terms: alternative, and more adequate *philosophical* means must be found.

More importantly, though, as Timpanaro himself recognizes elsewhere in his essay, Engels' role in the division of labour between Marx and himself was that of 'polemicizing with contemporary culture'. This means that Engels' work cannot be taken as the development of a scientific discourse, enshrouded in a mystifying, but dispensible, dialectical garb. The form it takes, the problems it poses, the means it employs, and the solutions it offers are all at least in part determined and constituted by the configurations of that 'contemporary culture'. Engels' texts are, in a sense, an 'interface' between the newly founded science of human history, contemporary developments in the natural sciences, and the broader cultural struggles between and within the major social antagonists of late nineteenth-century Europe: their forms of argument and mode of development cannot be expected to be identical with those of a scientific discourse. This is not, of course, to consign them to the dustbin of irredeemable ideological falsehood. Rather, it is to pose the problem – of great importance both intellectually and politically – of the status of those discourses which mediate between the sciences and popular ideological struggles.

To consider Engels' work in this way is already to expose as limited and one-sided the familiar point that the logic and epistemology of dialectical materialism may, and, indeed, has become an obstacle to scientific advance. Not only does this objection to Engels presuppose a questionable thesis about the determining role of epistemologies in the production of substantive scientific knowledge, but it entirely neglects the importance which philosophical reflection on the sciences may have for other social and cultural practices, as a form of mediation between them and the sciences. Where, for example, there are cultural and political struggles over the appropriation and/or suppression of new scientific knowledges, philosophical conceptions of science generally play an important part. If this is so, then Engels' work must be investigated not just in its consequences for the advance of the

sciences themselves, but also in its effectiveness as in intervention for or against specific appropriations of scientific
knowledge. Later in this paper I shall discuss in some detail
Engels' philosophical interventions against the 'vulgar'
materialist philosophical appropriation of mid-century physiology, and against certain forms of social Darwinism.

But before attempting this, it will be necessary to at least
sketch the elements of a general theoretical approach to the
analysis of articulations between scientific discourses and
popular cultural and political struggles. According to the
approach I shall adopt,[7] cultural struggles belong to a
relatively autonomous domain of social struggle, their terms,
forms and outcomes being partially, but *only* partially,
explicable in terms of other fields of struggle, and, in turn,
having definite effects on those other fields of struggle,
including the political. The field of struggle constituting
any specific conjuncture of a social formation will include a
definite configuration of diverse 'forms of social consciousness'. These forms of social consciousness are themselves
constituted by the characteristic social practices, rituals and
lived relationships of individuals, groups, classes, class-
alliances, and inter-class social movements. Such practices
and relationships have a symbolic, conceptual content. They
embody social meanings, which may be more or less explicit
in the discourses with which the practices are interwoven.
For any particular form of social consciousness, the universe of meanings embodied in its practices and relationships
may become the object of a distinctive social practice of
theoretical elaboration (examples: commercial practices of
late eighteenth-century competitive capitalism and the
theoretical discourse of classical political economy;
eighteenth-century bourgeois legal and political practices and
the political philosophy of the Enlightenment). In so far as
there is a conceptual unity and coherence between such
theoretical discourses and the social practices which are
their objects and social foundations, they may be referred to as
'theoretical ideologies', so long as it is remembered that there
can be no clear demarcation between a form of social consciousness in its theoretical and in its practical state.

The elaboration of theoretical ideologies is not the only

form of cognitive practice, however. I shall provisionally refer to sciences as cognitive practices which establish a conceptual discontinuity, or autonomy from the forms of social consciousness inhabiting the social formation in which they are constituted. This may be understood as, in part, an effect of the adoption within these social practices of rigorous rational rules for the production and correction of theoretical discourse. I should not here be understood as offering a definition of the sciences. I am, rather, relying on a more-or-less consensual ostensive characterization of certain disciplines as scientific (modern physics, chemistry, genetics, embryology, etc.), and drawing attention to one feature of their relationship to other discourses and practices – their conceptual autonomy – which is of interest for my present concerns.

This conceptual autonomy of the sciences, which is generally sustained by the institutional isolation of 'pure' scientific research both from immediate political control from 'above' and from diffusion among the mass of the population 'below', entails a more-or-less clear discontinuity between scientific discourses and those cultural forms whose patterns of alliance and conflict constitute the conjuncture.

From the standpoint of the dominant cultural forces, new scientific concepts are always potentially subversive: they are a potential challenge to the prevailing ideological configuration (Copernicus, Galileo, Darwin). Their popular diffusion necessitates some shift in the terms of the antagonisms which constitute that configuration. In the West, since the sixteenth and seventeenth centuries, the quite special congnitive authority of the sciences with almost all classes and social forces has entailed a major struggle over the cultural appropriation of each successive scientific innovation. For the eighteenth-century Enlightenment the authority of the Galilean-Newtonian conception of nature was claimed as the only firm intellectual basis for aesthetic, juridical, political and ethical philosophies of the greatest variety. In the nineteenth century new developments in physiology, embryology and geology all had their effects on popular culture, whereas evolutionary theory, in one form or another, established a near hegemony in late nineteenth-century social and political theory.

For the dominant cultural forces the subversive potential of scientific ideas is already harnessed by the very discontinuity of scientific discourse from popular forms of social consciousness, and its institutional containment within a specialist elite. But insofar as scientific ideas do attain a popular diffusion, the dominant political and cultural power may adopt a strategy of suppression, and/or of cultural struggle over the appropriation of the new scientific ideas. This frequently takes the form of a one-sided elaboration and articulation of scientific discourse to render it coherent with the dominant cultural forms. In some cases this amounts to more than a mere defensive neutralization of scientific innovation. It may, as in the case of imperialist appropriations of Darwinism, serve as an ethical legitimation of a major new political strategy of the power-bloc.

From the standpoint of the popular classes and social movements, new scientific ideas serve as a major source of ethical legitimacy. They furnish new resources for the critique of the established order, and new intimations of its impending transcendence. Examples of both of these are found in Engels' work. But, even more frequently, scientific advances remove the irrational bases for the authority of the established forms of social and political authority. (The Church, the monarchy, aristocratic privilege – all were the objects of forms of cultural opposition deriving much from both the content and the rational methodology of the sciences.)

All of this, however, presupposes that the autonomy of scientific discourse, the discontinuity between it and broader cultural struggles, may be bridged. The question of how this is achieved, of what is involved in the construction of 'mediating' discourses which effect the cultural appropriation of the sciences in the interests of the dominant or oppositional cultural forces is a question too much neglected, in my view, even within the Marxist tradition.

Throughout the nineteenth century, and especially, but not exclusively, in Germany the mediating discourse was a

species of philosophical discourse. Such philosophical movements as positivism, Romantic 'Naturphilosophie', the
'vulgar' materialism of Vogt, Moleschott, and Büchner,
Haeckelian 'monism', and dialectical materialism itself all
claimed a scientific foundation. All articulated their scientific derivations in a philosophical form, and all aimed at, and
achieved, an audience far wider that specifically intellectual
circles, even wider than the conventionally 'educated' classes.
What they offered was not merely an epistemological or
methodological reflection upon the sciences (although most
of them did *include* that). What they offered was a general
account of the nature and structure of the world, its inter-
connexions and forms of motion, as well as a conception of
the place of the human species in that world – its origins and
prospects. More than this, they offered a fellowship of
believers, institutional rituals and practices, and often the
missionary zeal of a secular religion. Despite the quasi-
religious character of most of these movements, their claims to
scientific foundation should be taken seriously. All of them
included in their memberships, or were founded by, scientific thinkers and 'lay' intellectuals of considerable scientific
literacy. It was principally through the efforts of movements
such as these that scientific ideas became diffused amongst the
popular classes. Finally, these movements were not confined
to education and edification; almost all of them had more-or-
less definite political objectives. It was, therefore, through
the diffusion of such 'mediating discourses' that the scientific
innovations of the nineteenth century came to play a material
role in the popular cultural and political struggles of the
period.

It is, then, this field of struggle, above all else, to which
Engels' dialectics of nature belongs, and it is in terms of this
general theoretical framework that I shall attempt to reassess
his philosophical achievements.

Engels' Conjuncture
When Marx, writing to Lassalle on 16 January 1861, echoes
Engels' welcome of Darwin's book, he described its achievement as two-fold. First, it dealt the 'death blow' to teleology in
the natural sciences. But, not only that, 'its [teleology's]

rational meaning is empirically explained'.[8] When one understands Darwin, one understands both the mechanism of the
origin of new species, *and* why previous biology had been
unable to conceive of such an origin other than through
teleology. Similarly, any adequate account of Engels' dialectic of errors must seek to understand not only the errors
but their 'rational meaning': What was it about Engels'
intellectual project that rendered a return to Hegel seem
necessary?

A condition of our satisfying this methodological requirement is that we first reconstruct the conjuncture into which
Engels' texts were an intervention. A conception of the
eventual unity of the sciences, natural and human, is present
from the early works of both Marx and Engels onwards.
Also persisting throughout the career of Engels, in particular,
is an interest in and concern with the latest developments in
scientific knowledge. In the correspondence, Engels often
introduces Marx to what he considers to be the most significant of the new scientific works and discoveries. But it was
not until, in Engels' own account, he gave up his business
activities and moved to London, in 1870, that he was able to
devote himself systematically to reading in the natural
sciences and mathematics. This work, according to the
Preface to *Anti-Dühring* had occupied him for 'the best part
of eight years', and the polemic against Dühring was a task
imposed upon him in the midst of that period. Again, on
Engels' own account, the work of criticizing Dühring was not
a task he willingly accepted. He was prevailed upon to under-
take it, not out of any recognition of the intellectual challenge
of Dühring, but for specifically political reasons: Dühring's
popularity and influence even within Social Democratic
circles threatened to be a new occasion for sectarian division
and confusion within a 'Party, which was still so young and
had but just achieved definite unity'.

That this political task – of 'critically examining' Herr
Dühring's would-be reform of socialism – required Engels to
take up positions in philosophy, mathematics, 'all things
under the sun and with some others as well', was, again, not a
product of Engels' choice. It was necessitated by the form of
Dühring's own work. 'The new socialist theory was presented

as the ultimate practical fruit of a new philosophical system. It was therefore necessary to examine it in its connection with this system, and in doing so to examine the system itself.'[9]

Further, Dühring was not alone in his system-building. Philosophical world-outlooks abounded in contemporary Germany, and, far from approving of this, Engels denounced the 'sublime nonsense' that results from dilettante speculation about the sciences. As to such tendencies within the Social Democratic Party itself, Engels regarded them as an 'infantile disease'.

So, in his very brief 'preface' to the first edition (1878) of *Anti-Dühring*, Engels identifies the causes of his intervention as political, as connected with the specific requirements of the German Social Democratic Party at a crucial period in its history, and the form it takes as required by the speculative and system-building character of the tendencies of thought against which he is aligned. I shall broadly follow Engels in these observations, attempting to characterize Engels' conjuncture in relation, first, to some of the more popular and influential nineteenth-century systems of philosophical and social thought which were associated with developments in the sciences, and, second, to the political conjuncture, especially in the German workers movement, of the 1870s and 1880s.

The Philosophical Conjuncture

I have already referred to philosophical 'world-views' as the principal form of mediating discourse between advances in the special sciences and broader cultural struggles. The 'Naturphilosophie' which permeated the German universities, under the influence of Hegel and Schelling at the end of the eighteenth century, and for the first decades of the nineteenth century, was distinctive in that it was primarily a philosophical incursion into science, rather than a popularizing discourse. The other major scientific philosophical system of the early nineteenth century, the 'positivisme' of St Simon and Comte, involved the derivation of a theory of the nature of 'man' and the social from a generalized theory of the nature and structure of the physical world. The major classes of fact – astronomical, physical, chemical, biological –

were ordered according to their mutual relations of dependence or autonomy, and this ordering in turn used to generate
an ordering of the sciences on the basis of their relations of
complexity/simplicity,   concreteness/abstraction,   depen-
dence/autonomy, etc. The science of the most dependent
class of phenomena, and therefore the most complex and
concrete was to be the science of the human species–
sociology.

Though nominally empiricist in its epistemology, positivism was far more than an epistemological reflection on the
natural sciences, and a programme for applying their methods
to the study of human society. It included a scientifically
based 'ontology', a theory of the nature and structure of the
world, together with the place of mankind in that world.
More even than this, it became an organized social and
political force, a secular religion with an international
following. In its main outlines the Durkheimian tradition in
French sociology derives from, and remains within, this
philosophical world-outlook.

Of more central relevance in defining Engels' philosophical
conjuncture were two 'waves' of post-Feuerbachian materialism[10] which achieved wide popular appeal especially in mid
and late nineteenth-century Germany. The first 'wave' of
materialism is represented by what Engels usually refers to as
the 'vulgar' materialism of Büchner, Vogt, and Moleschott.

Gregory's very important study of 'scientific' and 'dialectical' materialism[11] recognizes the connection of this
materialism of the 1840s and 1850s with the new developments in science, especially physiology, but he follows
Temkin[12] in referring to it as 'metaphysical' materialism as
distinct from the 'scientific' materialism of Du Bois Reymond
and the other physiologists, who were materialist principally
in their methodology. However, as I have tried to show
elsewhere,[13] the materialism of the new generation of German
physiologists was not merely methodological. Schwann
defined his research programme by means of a contrast
between two views on the fundamental powers of organized
bodies, the 'teleological' view, which he rejected, and the
preferable 'physical' view, according to which: ' ... the
fundamental powers of organized bodies agree essentially

with those of inorganic nature, that they work altogether blindly according to laws of necessity and irrespective of any purpose, that they are powers which are as much established with the existence of matter as the physical powers are.'[14] The materialism of this passage is an ontological doctrine—it concerns the nature and 'fundamental powers' of matter. The physiological methodology to be employed *follows from* this ontology, rather than, as in the earlier position of Müller, being advocated independently of any clear ontological commitment.

Nevertheless, Gregory is right in arguing that the 'vulgar' materialists extended the materialist approach of the physiologists beyond its scientific context into a philosophical world-view. Though the materialism of these popularizers owed much to Feuerbach, its close links with natural science were even more marked. Vogt and Moleschott were both physiologists, Vogt having held an academic position at Giessen until his removal for his revolutionary political activities between 1847 and 1849. Vogt was an advocate of the familiar eighteenth-century reductionist-materialist treatment of the mind–body problem: the soul is a product of the brain, which 'produces ideas as the liver produces bile and the kidneys urine'. Büchner and Moleschott were materialists of a more qualified stamp. Büchner's *Kraft and Stoff* (1855) advocated a dual ontology of matter and force, thought being treated as a force identical with that involved in other vital functions such as digestion. Moleschott, who had also been dismissed from his university post, in Heidelberg, for his views, combined a philosophical approach derived from Hegel with a generalization of the new materialist physiology to yield a confusedly materialist world-outlook.

All of these materialists were advocates, with more or less qualification, of a reductionist form of materialism, in the sense of the methodological doctrine of the explicability of all properties and behaviour of bodies–living and non-living, human and non-human–in terms of universal laws of matter. These laws, in turn, were generally supposed to be identical with those of Newtonian mechanics. This, as Gregory points out, generates intractable intellectual difficulties for their ethical and political doctrines, which were committed to the ideas of freedom and responsibility in action. Büchner held that the non-material manifestations of matter were determined by it, but not completely so, whilst Moleschott adhered to a notion of conformity to the laws of nature as an ethical ideal. In their religious views, all were anti-clerical, generally polemically so, advocating instead a secular religion of unity of the species with nature reminiscent of that of Feuerbach and the early Marx and foreshadowing certain aspects of Haeckel's 'monism'.

Also reminiscent of Feuerbach was the republicanism of the mid-century materialists. Büchner and Vogt were active in the events of 1848, and Vogt as delegate to the National Assembly even earned a word of commendation from Marx.[15] After the defeats of the period, however, they retreated either into exile, or into a purely propagandistic form of practice. Vogt's drift to the right and denunciation of the left led to a reply by Marx in the pamphlet *Herr Vogt*.

The second wave of popular materialism in Germany was occasioned by the reception of Darwin's *The Origin of Species*, which provided it with new natural scientific foundations. The mid-century materialists all responded enthusiastically to Darwin, and were joined by others – most notably by the leading German biologist, Ernst Haeckel. Vogt and Haeckel were amongst the first in Germany to publicly proclaim the conclusion which Darwin had deliberately avoided drawing in his *Origin*: the descent of the human species from primate stock by the operation of the same mechanisms which prevailed elsewhere in organic nature.

Though widely regarded and respected as an authority on biological questions, Haeckel was also a major founder and popularizer of social Darwinism as a 'monistic' world-outlook. Indeed, his commitment to evolutionary theory seems to have been primarily to it as a theory of the common descent and interconnectedness of living organisms, including mankind, and as a theory of progress through the 'struggle for life'. His promulgation of the supposed law that ontogeny recapitulates phylogeny as the 'fundamental law of organic evolution'[16] was a long way from Darwin's own careful treatment of embryological evidence as indicating the underlying kinship of the major groups of organisms.

Also a long way from Darwin, even in his later works, wa
Haeckel's emphasis on 'adaptation' as a mechanism of evo
lutionary change. Whereas Darwin's great innovation ha
been a conception of the formation of new species as the resul
of natural selection through the struggle for existence betwee
randomly occurring variations, there was no adequate theor
either of the causes of these variations or of the mechanism o
their inheritance. Indeed, on the currently most favoure
theory of inheritance, such variation would be blended ou
rather than transmitted to later generations. Added to thi
new estimates of the age of the earth, based on rates of cooling
suggested that the Darwinian mechanism was far too slow t
adequately account for organic evolution.

Haeckel was amongst those biologists who, in response t
these difficulties, resorted to neo-Lamarckian conceptions o
the inheritance of acquired adaptations to supplement, o
even replace, the distinctively Darwinian mechanism. Con
fusingly, Haeckel continued to use the term 'natural selec
tion', but as an approximate synonym for the 'struggle fo
existence', and was able even to advocate Lamarckianism
whilst claiming Darwinian orthodoxy: 'I hold, with Lamarc
and Darwin, that the hereditary transmission of acquire
characters is one of the most important phenomena i
biology'.[17]

The significance of the substitution of the Lamarckia
mechanism for the Darwinian one is that it makes possible th
fusion of the historicity of organic life, as disclosed by evo
lutionary theory proper, with the history of human cultura
and social life. If characteristics acquired, for example by us
and disuse, in the life of an individual organism, in its struggl
for existence, can be inherited by its offspring, and this is th
means by which progress occurs, then this mechanism i
equally applicable to the explanation of biological and huma
social history:

> The fact is that in this, as in all things, custom and adaptation t
> surrounding conditions determines the mode of life and soci
> arrangements of man as of other animals, and that this mode of lif
> becomes at last, by usage and habit, second nature. . . . Adaptatio
> and heredity, in their eternal mutual action and re-action, that i
> Natural Selection in the struggle for existence, are the etern

formative impulses, the Evolution forces, that give rise, by purely mechanical laws, to all the endless variety, both in the organization and modes of life of animals, and in their soul-life, the so-called instinct.[18]

One notable consequence of the fusion of the two historicities is Haeckel's biological representation of imperialist domination and actual genocide as (biologically) progressive. After pages of careful analysis of classification and anatomical comparison one is suddenly told that:

The immense superiority which the white race has won over the other races in the struggle for existence is due to Natural Selection, the key to all advance in culture, to all so-called history, as it is the key to the origin of species in the kingdoms of the living ... Of the ten species of man mentioned above, the first, primitive man, is dead this long time past. Of the nine others, the next four will pass in a shorter or longer time ... Even now these four races are diminishing day by day. They are fading away ever more swiftly before the o'ermastering white invaders. Melancholy as is the battle of the different races of man, much as we may sorrow at the fact that might rides at all points over right, a lofty consolation is still ours in the thought that, on the whole, it is the more perfect, the nobler man that triumphs over his fellows, and that the end of this terrific contest is in the vast perfecting and freedom of the human race, the free subordination of the individual to the lordship of reason.[19]

Gasman, in his valuable study of Haeckel's thought and influence, has gone so far as to say that Haeckel's evolution was a 'projection of German Romanticism and philosophical idealism'.[20] One does not have to accept this judgment in full to recognize the importance which Haeckel attached both to the broader philosophical and political implications of his biology, and to its popular dissemination. One finds throughout his work attempts to reinstate the scientific credentials of Lamarck, Goethe, Oken and the other speculative nature-philosophers, but the unified system of ideas which evolutionary theory makes possible in Haeckel's work is supposedly neither materialist nor idealist. 'Monism' is a philosophical doctrine which transcends the antagonism between one-sided materialism, and equally one-sided spiritism.[21] 'Force' and 'matter' are inseparably bound up with one another: 'There is spirit everywhere in nature, and we know of no

spirit outside of nature'. Whether materialist or not, Monism
was a form of mechanistic philosophy:

> The Monistic or Mechanical philosophy affirms that all the pheno-
> mena of human life and of the rest of nature are ruled by fixed and
> unalterable laws; that there is everywhere a necessary causal
> connection of phenomena; and that, therefore the whole knowable
> universe is a harmonious unity, a *monon*.

And, a little later:

> Thus the evolution of man is directed by the same 'eternal, iron
> laws' as the development of every other body. These laws always
> lead us back to the same simple principles, the elementary principles
> of physics and chemistry. The various phenomena of nature only
> differ in the degree of complexity in which the different forces work
> together.[22]

Following from this is the monist rejection of 'the common
antithesis of natural science and mental or moral science',[23]
and proclamation of the unity of science. Darwinism is itself
defended as an 'inductive' theory, a point on which Engels was
most severely critical of Haeckel.

Haeckel's treatment of the more specific question of the
mind–body relation is indistinguishable, but for its phylo-
genetic aspect, from that of Büchner's which I described
above: mental powers are a species of 'force', as much a
function of the brain as any other force is a function of a
material body. On the question of free will, Haeckel is as
radical as any materialist in denying its reality, but he does so
in a way that is distinctively evolutionary. ' . . . (our 'free'
volitions) are never really free, but always determined by
antecedent factors that can be traced to either heredity or
adaptation'.

This 'natural' interpretation of mankind, and 'spiritual'
interpretation of nature yields, then, not atheism, but a kind
of pantheistic religion of nature, and 'man's' unity with it
which has clear Romantic origins: 'Every science, as such, is
both natural and mental. That is a firm principle of Monism,
which, on its religious side, we may also denominate
Pantheism. Man is not above but in, nature'. But this naturalistic religion did not prevent Haeckel from sharing the anti-

clericalism of his predecessors, and his works contain many fine passages of polemics against the Church and religious dogma. It is perhaps this, together with his association with the International Free-thought movement which may have earned him his widespread reputation as a radical and progressive thinker. It is also worth noticing that Edward Aveling was amongst his English translators.

None of this, of course, explains why Haeckel's work demanded the repeated attention it in fact received from Engels (and, indeed, later Marxists). Amongst the intellectual reasons must have been the recognition in Social Democratic circles of the increasingly reactionary character of the cultural and political movements inspired by Haeckel and the other social Darwinists. How did this square with the eager acceptance Darwin's work had initially received from Marx and Engels? But more pressing than this intellectual problem was the great weight and authority of Haeckel's work with a remarkably wide public:

> Haeckel was able . . . to carry great weight and authority in matters outside the realm of science. Indeed it is safe to say that few men in modern times have had more of a general cultural influence than Haeckel. As the recognized spokesman of Darwinism in Germany he was taken as the virtually incontestable and exacting voice of science, both among many of the scientists and certainly among the general public.[24]

Haeckel's social Darwinism was, then, an influence which could not be ignored. It was a direct competitor with Social Democracy for the allegiance of the popular masses, especially in Germany.

The Political Context
During the 1860's Haeckel was a liberal and free-thinker, but, as Gasman points out, German liberalism tended to be more authoritarian and nationalistic than in the Western European countries. With the founding of the Bismarckian Second Empire in 1871, Haeckel, and German liberalism generally, shifted to the right. During the 1870s Haeckel supported Bismarck against the Catholic Church, and promulgated his evolutionary ethics and religion of nature as

an alternative modern and scientific basis for culture to supersede traditional ethics and Christianity. However, from the 1880s onwards it seems that Social Democracy came to be seen as the main threat to the German nation, and Haeckel argued on social Darwinist premises for the essentially aristocratic and undemocratic character of the laws of nature. Far from evolutionary monism representing a materialist step on the slope to Marxism, as Virchow had claimed, social Darwinism, was, in fact, the best defence against socialism.[25]

One of the most significant aspects in this rightward 'evolution' of Haeckel's social Darwinism was the centrality of the concept of the struggle for life and its application to the 'races' (or, for Haeckel, 'species') of mankind which lent itself to the requirements of German imperialism towards the close of the nineteenth century, and in the first decades of the twentieth century. Haeckel and his followers were closely aligned in these later years with the *Volkist* tradition, whose assertion of racial identity and romantic ideology of unity with nature, understood in a nationalistic sense, were to become an important source of Nazi ideology. Haeckel, by advocating Aryan superiority and strict racial eugenics served to lend the weight of scientific authority to the most reactionary currents in the German culture of the period.[26] Finally, in 1906, a Monist League, with Haeckel as its leader, was established, giving an organizational framework and political programme to what had hitherto been a diffuse, though powerful cultural movement.

The last three decades of the nineteenth century also saw the growth of the German workers' movement into a major political force. The unification of the two German working class parties under the Gotha programme in 1875 marked the beginning of a long period of steady growth of members and influence by the German Social Democratic Party. Though organizationally united, however, the party was politically divided and in a state of considerable theoretical confusion. According to Ryazanoff the pages of the party's central organ were 'often filled with the most grotesque mixture of various socialist systems'; also according to Ryazanoff, even Lieb-knecht confused Marxian materialist philosophy with that of

Moleschott and Büchner.[27] It was this state of theoretical and political confusion during the early years of the party which prompted both Marx's *Critique of the Gotha Programme* and Engel's *Anti-Dühring*.

Not only were many of the younger members of the party attracted by the scope, apparently scientific foundations, and vividness of Dühring's teachings, as against those of Marx and Engels, but the rivalries between followers of the previously independent workers' parties continued. Also not to be discounted was the influence within the ranks of social Democracy itself of the left wing of Haeckel's monist movement, some of whom advocated a common anti-clerical front with Social Democracy. It was above all the need to present a clear and systematic account of the distinctive features of his and Marx's views as a basis for unifying the German party, and counteracting competing influences, to which Engels' later philosophical writings, especially *Anti-Dühring*, were addressed.

Engels' Interventions

It is, then, not surprising that Engels should have returned to the philosophical system which had dominated his earlier years – that of Hegel – as the most promising source of a global and intellectually unified theoretical language for his responses to these intellectual challenges. As I hope to show, however, the unity bestowed by these appropriations of Hegel is a terminological unity only, and belies the underlying conceptual connections of Engels' thought. Those opponents of Engels who direct their fire at the Hegelian cover fail even to startle their prey.

In what follows I shall select two examples only of Engels' philosophical interventions – against mechanical materialism and against social Darwinism. I shall try to show that much, though not all, of what Engels has to say by way of critique of these currents of thought is both intellectually defensible, and statable in non-Hegelian, non-'dialectical' language without serious distortion or misrepresentation. In the course of doing so I hope also to illustrate the purely verbal character of the Hegelian systematicity and unity of Engels' interventions. But this is not to say that there remains no unity or systematicity in these works. On the contrary, I shall propose that Engels is the advocate of a form of systematic philosophical world-view, a form of 'scientific metaphysics', which is in important respects intellectually defensible.

Against Mechanical Materialism

It is widely recognized that one of the principal targets of Engels' philosophical writings was what he called mechanical or 'metaphysical' materialism. But this is usually defined solely in terms of its contrast with the 'dialectical' form of materialism advocated by Engels. There are, however, passages in which Engels defines mechanical materialism, as a strategy of explanation, without reference to its contrast with dialectics. In *Ludwig Feuerbach*, for example, it is defined as the 'exclusive application of the standards of mechanics to processes of a chemical and organic nature . . . '[28] In the notes to *Anti-Dühring* he gives a more extended and analytical account. Mechanics, he says, 'knows only quantities, it calculates with velocities and masses, and at most with volumes'.[29] Accordingly the 'mechanical approach explains all change from change of place (and) all qualitative differences from quantitative ones . . . '[30] Among the implications of this mechanical approach is that, if all qualitative differences and changes are to be 'reduced' to quantitative ones, to 'mechanical displacement, then we inevitably arrive at the proposition that all matter consists of *identical* smallest particles, and that all qualitative differences of the chemical elements of matter are caused by quantitative differences in number and by the spatial grouping of those smallest particles . . . '[31]

The French materialism of the eighteenth century was exclusively mechanical, according to Engels, and that form of materialism lives on in a 'shallow, vulgarized form' in the work of Büchner, Moleschott, and Vogt.[32] Further, Haeckel, too, fails to appreciate the philosophical significance of Darwinism, by representing its abolition of teleological or 'final' causes in evolution as entailing commitment to explanation by 'efficient', in the sense of 'mechanically acting' causes. There is sufficient evidence from the quotations presented above to indicate that, whether or not Haeckel was prepared to be regarded as a materialist, he was certainly committed to a form of mechanical reductionism in Engels' sense.

Engels presents arguments *ad hominem* both against these proponents of mechanical materialism, and against the 'mechanical approach' itself. First, against the 'vulgar' materialists, he argues that they are not aware of the consequence of their own doctrines: the thesis of the 'absolute qualitative identity of matter'. This is, in any case, a doctrine impossible to prove or disprove empirically. Whether Engels is committed to some form of verificationist or falsificationist critique here, or whether he simply intends to demonstrate the superficiality of the 'vulgar' materialists is unclear.

Against Haeckel's philosophical representation of Darwinism in terms of the 'narrow opposition' between efficient (= mechanical) and final causes, Engels argued that Hegel had already treated this as a 'superseded standpoint'. Engels' discussion on this point seems to suggest that modern science discloses forms of causality not to be grasped philosophically in terms of this opposition. Paradoxically, in the text of *Anti-Dühring*, he defends one such form of causality advocated by Haeckel himself from the criticism of Dühring. Haeckel's concept of 'adaptation' is criticized by Dühring as introducing a 'spiritistic confusion'. Engels argues that it is possible for forms of life to be 'purposively adapted', without there being involved any *conscious* purpose.[33] In modern terms, Engels may be represented as defending the use of functional explanations in biology, as distinct from both mechanical and teleological explanations.

More generally, Engels criticizes mechanistic materialism as a strategy by counterposing it to an approach which recognizes *both* the unity and interconnectedness of the subject-matters of the different sciences, *and* their relative distinctiveness and autonomy. What is involved here is a kind of natural scientific ontology of nature as a unified, though internally structured and differentiated whole, which Engels regards as preferable to the ontology implicit in mechanical reductionism. Against Dühring's, 'A single and uniform ladder of intermediate steps leads from the mechanics of pressure and impact to the linking together of sensations and ideas', Engels proposes a hierarchy of 'forms of motion' with transitions one to another which 'despite all gradualness' nevertheless constitute a 'leap, a decisive change'.[34] To express this 'leap' Engels makes use of the Hegelian notions of a 'nodal' point and the transformation of quantity into quality (and *vice versa*), but he doesn't *always* use this terminology. In a note to *Anti-Dühring*, for example, Engels comments on his own classification of the sciences in terms of his hierarchy of forms of motion as follows: 'If I term physics the mechanics of molecules, chemistry the physics of atoms, and furthermore biology the chemistry of albumens, I wish thereby to express the passing of any one of these sciences into one of the others, hence both the connection, the continuity, and the distinction, the discrete separation.'[35]

Elsewhere, Engels amplifies his notion of nature as a hierarchy of forms of motion by linking motion with the very nature of matter itself. Motion, he says, is 'the mode of existence, the inherent attribute' of matter, which is, in turn, 'unthinkable without motion'. The universe is a 'system', in the sense of 'an interconnected totality of bodies' in continuous interaction with one another.[36] The different domains of the universe are constituted by levels in the hierarchy of complexity of forms of motion, are demarcated by 'decided leaps', and form 'the basis for the separation' of the different sciences.[37] Since the investigation of motion had to begin with its simplest form, there is a definite ordering in the historical development of the different sciences, so that at any point in time, the different sciences will display great unevennesses in their levels of development.[38]

Engels' use of the Hegelian law of transformation of quantity into quality (and *vice versa*) in this context can be understood as a 'first approximation' to a concept of emergent qualities and laws, consequent upon a given level of organization, and requiring distinct concepts, language and methods for their characterization and investigation. Thus, in *Ludwig Feuerbach*, we get the admission that the 'standards' of mechanics are applicable to chemical and organic processes, 'but are pushed into the background by other, higher laws.'[39] The explanation of higher-level laws and properties in terms of lower ones is a feature of many of the epoch-making new developments in science (that is those which reveal 'interconnections' – the mechanical theory of heat, organic syntheses, atomic theory in chemistry, and so on), but this explanation cannot be assumed to be achieved without remainder: 'That the present tendency of science goes in this direction can be readily granted, but does not prove that this direction is the exclusively correct one, that the pursuit of this tendency will *exhaust* the whole of physics and chemistry.'[40]

Some notion, then, of the unity of nature, and, hence, of the sciences, can be sustained without concessions to a dualist absolute separation of domains of nature (living/non-living; mental/material), and also without concessions to a quite unnecessarily restrictive (because it *forecloses* questions which remain open for future scientific research) mechanical materialism. That Engels commits himself to the characterization of this conception of the unity of nature and of the sciences in terms derived from Hegelian dialectical philosophy is unfortunate not only because Hegel's categories are applied quite externally and inessentially, but also because the same categories are also used, quite confusingly, by Engels, to make other points. For example, the quantitative/qualitative distinction is used in its least 'forced' application when Engels deals with the relationship between physics and chemistry, and where there is a resonance between this distinction and that between primary and secondary qualities. But the distinction is quite unhelpful, for example, in characterizing the 'transition' from chemistry to biology, and is, further, used to make a quite distinct point in relation to changes of state, which are *physical* processes, and which are comprehended within the confines of a single science.

The second major objection to mechanical materialism (as also to *Naturphilosophie*) is its ahistorical character. Mechanical materialism recognizes 'development in time' in human history, but not in nature.[41] The existence of mere motion and change in nature was not, of course, denied by the older philosophy, and Engels has difficulty stating in what the historical conception consists. In *Ludwig Feuerbach*, the Kant-Laplace hypothesis, geology, and the theory of

organic evolution are advanced in support of the historica
conception of nature, the last named being explained as 'the
conception that the animate natural beings of today are the
result of a long sequence of development from the simple to
the complex'.[42] What seems to be essential here is the notion
of history as development, and development in a definite
direction.[43] But the introduction into his characterization of
the historical process of the notion of levels of complexity
also suggests a historicization of the problem of 'emergence'
dealt with above. Historicity in nature is, in other words, the
emergence, in temporal succession, of new levels of complexity in forms of motion. This, indeed, is involved in the sketch
for a history of the world which Engels presents in the Introduction to the *Dialectics of Nature*. The domain of nature with
which each science deals represents not only a distinct level of
complexity of motion, but also a definite stage in the historica
evolution of the universe. Historicity in this sense, as much as
motion itself, must be regarded as an essential characteristic of
nature – beings are to be thought of as constantly in process of
change, of coming into being and passing away. This is true
not just of individual beings (for example disassociation of
organic beings on death) but also of whole domains of nature
(for example the origin of life out of inorganic processes, and
its eventual demise). Here, then, mixed up with a philosophically dubious quasi-teleological notion of historicity as
progressive development, there is also an attempt to confront
the problem of the emergence of new forms and structures as a
specifically historical problem. Engels is alive to the analogies
to be drawn between the production of new forms (qualitative leaps) in the history of nature, in the history of human
societies, and in the history (both organic and psychological)
of individual living things. That Engels suggests, by his
indifferent application of the dialectical laws of the transition
of quantity into quality, and negation of negation, to all of
these histories, that they may share not just an analogous, but
a *common* historicity is, to say the least, unfortunate. But the
importance of the analogies, as an epistemological resource
for the development of the science of human history is a baby
that need not be thrown out with the apparently reductionist bath-water. Indeed, I shall argue a little later that

surprisingly enough, Engels does recognize that nature and human society do not share a common historicity, the looseness of his appropriation of the dialectic notwithstanding.

But before I approach the question of Engels' treatment of the bearing of the natural sciences upon specifically human history, it is necessary to deal with the question of the status of the ontology which Engels counterposes to that of mechanical materialism. Isn't my exposition of Engels on this question a further demonstration of the aptness of the dismissal of Engels as a pre-critical metaphysician? There is a reasonably well-established distinction in contemporary philosophy between 'revisionary' and 'descriptive' metaphysics.[44] The latter differs from pre-critical, or revisionary metaphysics in its eschewal of the reforming zeal of its speculative sister. Descriptive metaphysics seeks only to derive the fundamental categories of commonsense thought by analysis of the presuppositions of everyday linguistic practices. If Engels' ontological theory is metaphysical, it is clearly not a metaphysics of either of these two forms. It is not speculative, but (in some as-yet undefined sense) 'based on' scientific knowledge, and, since scientific knowledge transcends the categories of commonsense thought, it cannot be a descriptive metaphysics either. Engels' ontology is the product of philosophical reflection on what is presupposed by the recent development of the sciences. The convergence, the realignment, of whole fields of theory which had previously developed separately (organic/inorganic chemistry, mechanics/theory of heat, etc.) is unintelligible, as is the replacement of one theory by another within the same specialism, unless these different fields of theoretical discourse are apprehended as so many attempts at knowledge of a unitary though internally differentiated, natural universe. This unity of nature is an essential precondition for convergence of the sciences, for the repeated discovery of 'interconnections', whilst the differentiation of nature is implied by the discreteness and uneven historical development of the different sciences. The unity of nature is, further, presupposed in Engels' normative methodology, which rules out the promulgation of mutually 'incompatible' laws in different domains.

The detailed contents of Engels' ontology do, of course, involve a degree of speculation. They go beyond what is established in the science of his day. They do not *belong* to scientific discourse, as such. They involve, for example, abstraction from the historically produced unevennesses of that contemporary scientific conjuncture. Where different sciences do presuppose incompatible ontologies, or where the ontology of the science is still controversial, Engels abstracts and simplifies in the interests of the presentation of a coherent conception of the totality.

It is beyond the scope of this paper to deal at all comprehensively with the philosophical problems posed by such a 'scientific metaphysics'. However, some brief indicators of its status can be given. First, recent work in this country, in the tradition of 'realist' philosophy of science, has points of contact with Engels' philosophical enterprise. Bhaskar's 'transcendental' realism argues for the philosophical legitimacy of arguments from the character of rational procedures in science (for example experimentation) to conclusions of a very general kind about the nature of the world as presupposed in the rationality of those procedures.[45] I have myself tried to show that the intelligibility of 'cross-paradigm' discourse, even in the extreme case of incommensurability of 'paradigms', depends on the notion of a common extra-discursive reality to which each 'paradigm' makes reference, though by means of different, and incompatible, complexes of concepts.[46]

Engels' scientific metaphysics includes arguments and conclusions of this general type, but it goes beyond this to represent in a unified and more-or-less coherent form a detailed ontology based on current substantive knowledge in the different sciences. Engels is here doing no more than generalizing from procedures employed by scientists themselves in bringing to bear discoveries in one discipline upon controversies in an adjacent one, but this generalization of the procedure results in a quite distinct type of theoretical structure (a 'world-view') and discourse.

As to this aspect of Engels' scientific metaphysics, its legitimacy is less easily established. Must one say that it is a form of discourse imposed on Engels, not by the nature of his intellectual project as such, but by the character of his, ultimately political, task of cultural-struggle with other tendencies of thought which were similarly presented as systematic world-outlooks? This is what Timpanaro seems to think, and certainly Engels' appropriation of Hegelian categories such as the qualitative – quantitative distinction to give unity to his solutions to quite distinct problems is certainly best understood in these terms. On the other hand, if the elaboration of philosophical world-outlooks was the characteristic way in which, for a whole culture during a certain period, the discoveries of the sciences were introduced into popular discourse, then questions may be asked about whether different specific attempts to do this may be compared or ranked in terms of the adequacy with which they achieve it. There may, in other words, be argument-forms, criteria of appraisal, validity, and so on, specific to these mediating discourses, being distinct both from those of the sciences, and from those currently recognized in the analytical tradition in philosophy. If this approach is adopted, then one has to appraise Engels' work not in terms of the contrast between formal and dialectical logic, or between speculative metaphysics and epistemology, but rather in terms of the contrast between Engels' ontology and methodology of the sciences and those provided by, for example, Comte, the 'vulgar' materialists and the social Darwinists. If there is *some* sense in Engels' claim that the development of the sciences in the nineteenth century has revealed fundamental features of the universe, and carries methodological implications which are grasped *neither* by mechanistic materialism, nor by its nineteenth-century legatees, then maybe one owes it to Engels to give a better account of what it is. If there is *some* sense in Engels' claim that Haeckel's philosophical representation of evolution as an 'induction' is fundamentally at variance with the methodological implications of evolutionary theory, if his claim that Haeckel's use of the 'simple opposition' between mechanical (= efficient) and final causes fails to grasp the significance of new developments in the sciences has *some* point, then surely *our* task must be to say what that point is, rather than dismiss both Engels and Haeckel as 'metaphysicians'?

Engels himself never falls into this way of criticizing others. That eighteenth-century materialism combined a sound, but limited basis in scientific knowledge with non-sensical speculation was inevitable, Engels thought, given the levels of development, in the eighteenth century, of the sciences themselves. Speculation, as a source of knowledge-claims independent of and alongside of the special sciences is not demonstrated by Engels to be, as such, and in general, methodologically unsound, so much as superseded by the nineteenth-century development of science itself. The systematizing and generalizing work of philosophy now has an adequate basis in science itself: science 'absorbs' philosophy.[47]

Engels against Social Darwinism

That Engels should have opposed social Darwinist forms of biological reductionism is in some ways surprising. In biological doctrine Engels tended to follow Haeckel's neo-Lamarckianism rather than Darwinism as it is now generally understood, and I have already tried to show that the Lamarckian mechanism for speciation opens the way for biological reductionism.[48] In addition to this, I have tried to show that the indifferent application of categories of the 'dialectic' to different domains in nature can give the impression that human history and the history of organic nature can be understood through identical philosophical (dialectical) categories.[49] There is, perhaps, a further temptation to collapse the distinction between these two historicities by extending the notion of 'struggle for life' beyond its specific meaning to refer to one feature of the process of natural selection, to apply it not to competition between individual human beings or to races and nations, as social Darwinist thought had done, but to struggle between the classes.

There is clear evidence from Engels' notes that his adoption of neo-Lamarckianism in evolutionary theory did indeed lead him into biological reductionism on occasion. For example, in the notes to *Anti-Dühring* he argues that natural science has transformed the conception of the subject of experience for epistemology from the individual to the 'genus', through the notion of inheritance of acquired characteristics: 'If, for instance, among us the mathematical axioms seem self-evident to every eight-year-old child, and in no need of proof from experience, this is solely the result of 'accumulated inheritance'. It would be difficult to teach them by a proof to a Bushman or Australian Negro'.[50] Similar passages are also to be found in Engels' essay on 'The Part Played by Labour in the Transition from Ape to Man', which relies quite explicitly on the Lamarckian evolutionary mechanism.[51] There also is some evidence of both Marx and Engels submitting to what I referred to above as the 'temptation' to bring class-struggle under the extended concept of struggle for life.[52]

But the great weight of the work of both Marx and Engels on the relationship of Darwinism to human history *both* asserts the relevance and importance of the former to the latter, *and* rejects the reduction of the latter to the categories of the former. The conception of the world as an interconnected unity, together with Darwinism's authoritative extension of the historical conception of nature constitute the *relevance* of Darwinism to human history. Simultaneously, the autonomy of human history both follows from the metaphysical conception of nature as internally structured and differentiated, and is evident from a rigorous analysis of the adequacy and scope of the concepts belonging to the theory of organic evolution.

Marx's general opposition to social Darwinist reductionism is evident, for example, in his letter to Kugelmann, where Marx opposes Lange's collapsing together of Darwinian and human social historicity under the phrase 'struggle for life'.[53] Marx's very condensed critique appears to have three distinct aspects. First, whatever the 'struggle for life' is, in human societies, it must be examined concretely in relation to each historical form of society. There can be no direct subsumption of all concrete historical struggles under a single law. Secondly, for Lange, the content given to the concept of the struggle for life is the Malthusian 'population fantasy', which Marx rejects. Finally, for Lange, and by implication, other social Darwinists who follow the same logical course, concepts such as 'struggle for existence', detached from their specific scientific setting are reduced to the status of a mere 'phrase'. The unity of human and organic historicities is, in other words, not recognized through a unification of theoretical discourses, but merely *verbally*, through the appropriation of a *phrase*.

As Timpanaro has shown,[54] social Darwinism involves a double conceptual 'movement': first the Malthusian theory of population is extended from capitalist society to organic nature, in the form of the theory of struggle for existence and natural selection, and then the reverse 'movement' of ideas asserts these mechanisms as universal laws of human society. According to Timpanaro, both Marx and Engels criticize the second movement, but Engels has doubts from the beginning about even the first.[55] I shall not, in fact, investigate the question of the supposed extension of Malthus to organic nature by Darwin, but focus instead on the reverse, properly social Darwinist, 'movement'. However, an apparent problem for one of Engels' lines of attack on social Darwinism is that it seems to presuppose the adequacy of the extension of certain of the concepts of bourgeois political economy to organic nature.

I suggested above[56] that new scientific theories may become an important source of ethical critiques of the established order and its culture. One of Engels' favourite arguments against the social Darwinists is to say that the discovery of the same laws in organic nature as political economy discovers in bourgeois society, far from legitimating this form of society, demonstrates its backwardness and the necessity for its transcendence:

> Darwin did not know what a bitter satire he wrote on mankind, and especially on his countrymen, when he showed that free competition, the struggle for existence, which the economists celebrated as the highest historical achievement, is the normal state of the *animal kingdom*.[57]

And in a letter to F.A. Lange:

> I too was struck, the very first time I read Darwin, with the remarkable likeness between his account of plant and animal life and the Malthusian theory. Only I came to a different conclusion from yours: namely, that nothing discredits modern bourgeois develop-

ment so much as the fact that it has not yet got beyond the economic forms of the animal world.[58]

But this ethical critique of capitalist social relations loses its force if the parallel between bourgeois society and organic nature can be shown to be mistaken, and Engels *does* argue that it is mistaken.

Is this ethical critique of social Darwinism, then, purely *ad hominem*, and inconsistent with what Engels says elsewhere, or can it be reconciled with the generally non-reductionist position of Marx and Engels? In his less guarded statements of the ethical critique (the first quotation above is an example) Engels does write as if there were an *identity* between the laws of bourgeois society and organic nature, but in his more guarded statements of it (see the second quotation above) he merely refers to a 'likeness'. The existence of suggestive, though incomplete parallels between the two domains is quite consistent with both the ethical critique, and non-reductionism. That the latter is Engels' position is clear from the context even of the first, apparently reductionist quote. Engels is at his most apparently reductionist when he is emphasizing the contrast between bourgeois society and a future socialist society characterized by the 'conscious organization of social production'.[59] But even here Engels argues that production in general has already lifted mankind as a species 'above the rest of the animal world'.

There is, then, in Engels, not only a reservation about the 'unconditional' applicability of the categories of Malthusian population theory to organic nature, but also a two-fold rejection of the reverse movement to yield 'eternal natural laws of society'.[60] First, there is a discontinuity within organic nature between the human species and the rest of 'the animal world' which is established with production as a distinctively human form of activity. In the Notes to *Dialectics of Nature*, and in his letter to Lavrov, Engels makes this point by way of a contrast between, at most, 'collection', which is the means by which other animals achieve their subsistence, and 'production', by which human beings prepare means of life which nature of itself would not have prepared.[61] It is the process of coming into being of this

distancing of the human species from other animals that
Engels describes in terms of Lamarckian evolution in the
'Part Played by Labour'. But notwithstanding the biological
character of the mechanism which explains the genesis of the
new phase in the history of the world, Engels is quite clear
that once it is established its further history cannot be understood in biological terms only. The significance of the collection – production distinction is that it 'makes impossible any
immediate transference of the laws of life in animal societies to
human ones'.[62]

But here the second aspect of Engels' critique emerges.
Not only is there a discontinuity at the boundaries of the
human and the non-human within organic nature, there are
further discontinuities *within* the human, discontinuities,
which, like that between the human and the non-human, have
historical dimension. With each new phase of specifically
human development, a new situation arises as to the relationship between the social and the biological, and hence, as to the
applicability of biological concepts to the interpretation of
social relationships and their transformations. Even if such
concepts as 'the struggle for existence' continue to have a limited and conditional applicability after the establishment of
production, production itself soon brings about a new phase of
human development which rules out even this conditional
applicability: 'The struggle for existence – if we permit this
category for the moment to be valid – is thus transformed
into a struggle for pleasures, no longer for mere means of
subsistence but for means of *development*, *socially produced*
means of development, and to this stage the categories
derived from the animal kingdom are no longer applicable.'[63]
But this phase of human development, which coincides with
the existence and struggle of social classes, produces its own
transcendence when its highest form – capitalist society –
bursts its self-imposed barriers to the development of human
productive powers: 'The struggle for existence can then
consist only in this: that the producing class takes over the
management of production and distribution from the class
that was hitherto entrusted with it but has now become in-
competent to handle it, and there you have the socialist
revolution'. For the phase of human history which Engels

identifies with the existence of classes and class struggles, then, the notion of 'struggle for existence' still has some resonance as a metaphor, but '(even) the mere contemplation of previous history as a series of class struggles suffices to make clear the utter shallowness of the conception of this history as a feeble variety of the "struggle for existence"'.

The further, future, phase of human existence constituted in the transcendence of capitalist society by the operation of the mechanism of class struggle will abolish even the metaphorical application of the phrase 'struggle for existence'. The conscious and planned character of social production and distribution will raise mankind above the other animals 'as regards the social aspect' as did production in general 'as regards their aspect as a species'.[64]

In fact, this whole argument can be represented as a more detailed working-out of the rather condensed critique of social Darwinism presented by Marx in his letter to Kugelmann:[65] human history can be forced into the mould of biological categories only at the cost of reducing those categories to the status of mere 'phrases' which lack explanatory content, and are likely to be positively misleading. In Engels, the argument is presented by way of identifying a series of historically emerging discontinuities both within organic nature and within human society. Each new phase of existence is generated by the operation of the laws and mechanisms of the previous phase, but, once constituted, represents a new form of existence with its own laws and mechanisms which require new concepts and explanatory theories. The autonomy this achieves is, however, conditional and limited. The newer and more complex phases have both internal and external conditions of existence. Their persistence depends upon the continued operation of the laws and mechanisms of the earlier phases.[66]

It is clear, then, that Engels (as well as Marx) was able to mount a sustained and not obviously incoherent critique of social Darwinism despite his acceptance of Haeckel's neo-Lamarckianism, and despite a *philosophical* subsumption of the historicity of natural and human history under identical categories of the dialectic. How was this possible? One obvious answer to this question is that opposition to social

Darwinism was necessitated by the *politically* reactionary character of the predominant appropriations of Darwin. The critique of social Darwinism is thus an *ad hoc* and opportunist response to political imperatives. But there are reasons for not adopting this interpretation. First, opposition to reductionism is not the only, or even the most obviously effective, rebuttal of social Darwinism. Various forms of left-wing reductionism were possible, and, as we have seen, Marx and Engels seem to have been tempted in this direction on occasion.[67] Perhaps more significantly, though, even before 1859, and certainly before the predominantly reactionary character of social Darwinism was established, Engels was asserting not only the unity of mankind and the other animals, but also the 'qualitative' discontinuity between them.[68]

Finally, the theoretical unity of this critique of social Darwinism with the rest of Engels' scientific metaphysics is a further powerful argument against the representation of it as a mere *ad hoc* response to political imperatives. It does not, for Engels, follow from the recognition that both nature and human society are 'dialectical' in the sense of 'historical', that they share a common form of historicity. As distinct, and relatively autonomous domains within a unitary universe, distinct concepts and laws are required for their explanation. The Hegelian conception of a 'qualitative leap in a quantitative series', despite its evident defects, at least saves Engels from the reductionist errors that might have followed from a simple-minded application of the dialectic, and which *did* follow from neo-Lamarckianism in the case of Haeckel, but *not* in the case of Engels.

It is now possible to represent Engels' epistemological (anti-inductionist) and metaphysical (anti-mechanist) critique of Haeckel as merely complementing at the more abstract level, the critique of social Darwinism which Engels achieves more concretely through his analysis of the relationships between the concepts of struggle for existence, collection–production, class-struggle, and so on. Moreover, the metaphysical critique is deepened and strengthened by the more concrete argumentation, which serves to rebut any suggestion that the metaphysics is merely speculative.

Conclusion

I have attempted to show, by way of two examples, that Engels' later work on philosophy and the natural sciences can be understood as a series of interventions against specific tendencies of thought which were identified by Engels as significant targets for criticism in the intellectual and political conjuncture of late nineteenth-century Europe, and Germany in particular. These interventions concern the interface between popular cultural struggles, historical materialism as a theoretical discourse, and the natural sciences. More specifically, Engels' philosophical work, as well as contributing to the elaboration of an epistemology and methodology adequate to the requirements of scientific advance in the latter part of the nineteenth century, also seeks to provide the philosophical basis for a non-reductionist and progressive popular appropriation of new developments in the natural sciences. It is in this context that the confrontation with social Darwinism is to be understood. I have also illustrated, but not fully demonstrated that the appropriation of the Hegelian terminology and 'laws of the dialectic' plays a relatively superficial role in lending an appearance of overall unity to Engels' interventions on these questions. It is my view that this appropriation of Hegelian terminology and styles of argumentation was dictated largely by the character of the world-outlooks against which Engels polemicized, and by the philosophical resources then available to him. There is, nevertheless, an underlying philosophical unity in Engels' interventions, and it is one which is capable of intellectual justification.

The question, however, remains, given that our situation is very different from that faced by Engels, what, if anything, remains of importance in his philosophical work? I shall briefly mention three areas in which, it seems to me, philosophical work, building from what is viable in Engels, is an urgent necessity today.

First, although new scientific knowledge today is not, in general, appropriated and introduced into popular discourses in the form of philosophical world-outlooks, it nevertheless remains a powerful source of new ideological currents, or for the renewal of old ones. The 'mediating discourses' of today hardly compare in intellecutal stature or pretentions with those of the nineteenth century, but they are no less important as social and cultural forces. Genetics and animal ethology have both provided raw materials for a series of modern conservative and outright reactionary interventions into popular culture,[69] and there is not a little confusion on the left as to how to combat these interventions. Does one mount elaborate critiques of the theoretical basis of these 'mediating discourses' in the natural sciences, or is this to enter the terrain of the enemy? Should the strategy, rather, be to assert the autonomy of the human and the social as the most effective counter to reductionism? This latter strategy is one that either explicitly, or by default, has predominated among the West European and U.S. left in recent years.[70] A common feature of the various currents of 'Western Marxism' has been the avoidance of mechanistic or reductionist materialism at the cost of a lapse into neo-Kantian or other forms of dualism as the philosophical basis for the theory of history. Engels' modern materialism attempted both to avoid reductionism *and* to establish the relevance and real bearing of natural scientific knowledge to the understanding of the human species, its limits and possibilities. To sacrifice, on dualist metaphysical premises, the whole terrain of the natural sciences to conservative appropriations is not at all the only alternative to reductionism. Engels provides us with object lessons, both positive and negative, in how to develop a non-reductionist critique of reactionary appropriations of scientific knowledge which also makes available new knowledge to popular and progressive social forces.

Secondly, the development of 'crises' of a broadly ecological kind – world shortages of food and raw materials, the so-called 'energy crisis', new and potentially more devastating forms of pollution, and so on – in the current world situation is associated with proliferating theoretical and political responses. So far, the organized left has shown itself both politically and intellectually inadequate to the tasks imposed both by the crisis itself, and by the more-or-less spontaneous growth in several countries of an 'ecology' movement. This is a paradox, given the roots of the Marxist movement in a recognition of the central importance of

material productive practice, both in human historical
development, and in the relations between the forms of
human society and their external, 'natural', conditions of
existence. The dualism of so much modern Marxist theory
shows itself in the near-exclusive attention to the internal
conditions for the maintenance and reproduction of social
formations, at the expense of any serious analysis of the
external – biological, physical, chemical geographical, etc. –
sustaining conditions and conditions of reproduction of
specific forms of social life. It is true that human transformative practices incorporate our natural environment into
an internal condition of social existence, so that to a degree,
and in certain respects, the human species and its natural
environment are subject to a common history. But it must
also be emphasized, as Engels knew, that the natural world –
organic and inorganic – also has its own autonomous historicity, interconnected, though not fused, with that of human
societies. If this is so, then questions must be posed, and
answered, concerning the compatibility or otherwise of the
different actual and potential forms of social existence and
systems of production with their external conditions of
existence in organic and inorganic nature. Both dualist and
reductionist materialist philosophical premises are obstacles
to the adequate posing of such questions. Socialist theory and
practice is thus deprived of a major resource for reorienting
its relationship in a constructive way to autonomous movements such as those against environmental destruction,
women's oppression and racialism.

Finally, the recent emergence and influence of new forms
of idealism within the Marxist tradition itself[71] has made
necessary a re-examination of the philosophical and methodological requirements for the further development of historical
materialism itself. But that is for another day.

Notes

1   See, for example, G. Lichtheim, *Marxism* (London 1967), especially pt. 5.

2   An example of such a defence of Engels is J. Hoffman, *Marxism and the Theory of Praxis* (London 1975). One among the many Marxist critiques of Engels' 'metaphysics' is R. Gunn, 'Is nature dialectical?' in *Marxism Today* (Feb. 1977), pp. 45–52. The most renowned non-Marxist critique of dialectical philosophy is K. R. Popper, 'What is dialectic?', reprinted as ch. 15 of *Conjectures and Refutations* (London 1976).

3   Even Lucio Colletti, whose work on Engels [see especially his *Marxism and Hegel*, L. Garner (tr.) (London 1973) and 'Marxism and the dialectic', *New Left Review*, 93, pp. 3–29] is otherwise exemplary, does not satisfy this requirement. He is able effectively to expose the idealist philosophy of Nature which is implicit in any thoroughgoing application of the Hegelian dialectic to the natural world, but he is unable to explain how Engels could have become committed to so obviously a self-defeating intellectual programme. More specifically, Colletti's own simple distinction between contradiction and 'real opposition' is quite inadequate to conceptualize the complexity and diversity of kinds of causality disclosed by the modern natural and historical sciences. It was Engels' recognition of this complexity and diversity that was at the root of his anti-empiricism and his opposition to mechanical materialism and social Darwinism. The very simplicity of Colletti's distinction renders him incapable of understanding the point of Engels' interventions on these subjects. [See also Ted Benton, *Philosophical Foundations of the Three Sociologies*. (London 1977), pp. 60–1].

4   G. Stedman Jones, 'Engels and the end of classical German philosophy', *New Left Review*, 79 (May/June 1973), pp. 17–36.

5   S. Timpanaro, *On Materialism* (London 1975), especially ch. 3.

6   *Ibid*, p. 92. Gareth Stedman Jones (*op. cit.*) too, emphasizes the importance of the emergence of a historical perspective in the natural sciences to any understanding of Engels' later works. In particular, according to Stedman Jones, Engels was affected by the creation, in the nineteenth century, of historical sciences, developmental sciences, and sciences of interconnection. Although Stedman Jones is right in recognizing the importance of the concepts of history, development and interconnection in Engels' work on the sciences, I can find no justification for linking the concepts with a classification of the sciences. Rather, Engels refers to specific scientific advances – such as cell-theory or evolutionary theory – as each illustrating some, or all, of

these aspects of modern scientific knowledge. What is important, then, in characterizing Engels' *scientific* conjuncture, is not so much the creation of new sciences, but rather, a series of specific advances, each of which has a variety of radiating implications, both creating the conditions of further advance and rendering obsolete seveteenth- and eighteenth-century philosophical conceptions of science and nature.

7   For a more extended account, see my *Philosophical Foundations of the Three Sociologies op. cit.*, especially chs. 8 and 9 and *Radical Philosophy*, IX (Winter 1974), pp. 27–8.

8   K. Marx and F. Engels, *Selected Correspondence* (Moscow 1965), p. 123. Parenthesis added.

9   F. Engels, *Anti-Dühring* (London 1969), pp. 9–12.

10   See Timpanaro, *op. cit.*, pp. 81ff.

11   F. Gregory, 'Scientific and dialectical materialism', *Isis*, LXVIII. no. 242 (June 1977), pp. 206–23. See also F. Gregory, *Scientific Materialism in Nineteenth Century Germany* (Boston 1977), for a quite excellent treatment of this element in Engels' philosophical conjuncture.

12   O. Temkin, 'The idea of descent in post-Romantic Germany biology: 1848–58', in Glass, Temkin and Strauss, *Forerunners of Darwin: 1745–1859*. Temkin is, nevertheless, right in distinguishing between these two forms of materialism. They differ, though, in the specific ontological questions they confront, rather than in the concern of the physiological materialists with methodological reduction only.

13   E. Benton, 'Vitalism in nineteenth century scientific thought', *Studies in History and Philosophy of Science*, V, no. 1 (1974), pp. 17–48.

14   T. Schwann, *Microscopical Researchers*, H. Smith (tr.) (London 1847), p. 190.

15   K. Marx and F. Engels, *Collected Works*, VII (London 1977), p. 235.

16   E. Haeckel, *The Evolution of Man*, J. McCabe (tr.) (London 1906), I, ch. 1. For Darwin's treatment of embryological evidence see, for example, C. Darwin, *The Origin of Species* (Harmondsworth 1968), pp. 419–28.

17   E. Haeckel, *op. cit.*, p. 349, See also vol. I, ch. 5, of the same work.

18   E. Haeckel, 'On the division of labour in the life of nature and of man', a lecture to the Berlin Artisans' Association, 1868, included in *The Pedigree of Man and Other Essays*, E. B. Aveling (tr.) (London 1883), p. 98.

19   E. Haeckel, *ibid*, p. 85.

20   D. Gasman, *The Scientific Origins of National Socialism* (London and New York 1971), p. xxi.

21   E. Haeckel, *The Evolution of Man*, *op. cit.*, p. 356.

22   E. Haeckel, *ibid*, p. 357.

23   E. Haeckel, *ibid*, p. 356.

24   D. Gasman, *op. cit.*, p. xxii.

25   D. Gasman, *ibid*, ch. 5, see also V. Gerratana, 'Marx and Darwin', *New Left Review*, 82 (Nov./Dec. 1973) pp. 60–82.

26   See Gasman, *ibid*, Introduction.

27 D. Ryazanoff, *Karl Marx and Friedrich Engels* (London, no date), p. 207.

28 F. Engels, 'Ludwig Feuerbach and the end of classical German philosophy', Marx and Engels, *Selected Works*, II (London 1953), p. 338.

29 F. Engels, *Anti-Dühring, op. cit.*, pp. 442–3.

30 *Ibid*, p. 443, my parenthesis.

31 *Ibid*, p. 444.

32 F. Engels, 'Ludwig Feuerbach . . . ', *op. cit.*, pp. 337–8. See also Engels' review included in Marx's *Contribution to the Critique of Political Economy* (London 1971), p. 223.

33 Engels, *Anti-Dühring, op. cit.*, p. 89.

34 *Ibid*, p. 83.

35 *Ibid*, p. 442.

36 F. Engels, *Dialectics of Nature*, C. Dutt (tr. and ed.), Preface and Notes by J. B. S. Haldane (London 1941), pp. 35–6.

37 *Ibid*, p. 29.

38 *Ibid*, p. 35.

39 Engels, 'Ludwig Feuerbach . . . ', *op. cit.*, p. 338.

40 Engels, *Anti-Dühring, op. cit.*, p. 443.

41 Engels, *Dialectics of Nature, op. cit.*, p. 6.

42 Engels, 'Ludwig Feuerbach . . . ' *op. cit.*, p. 339.

43 See, for example, Engels' critical comment on Lyell's geology in *Dialectics of Nature, op. cit.*, p. 10fn.

44 See, for example, P. F. Strawson, *Individuals* (London 1964), p. 9ff.

45 R. Bhaskar, *Realist Theory of Science* (Hassocks 1978).

46 T. Benton, *Philosophical Foundations of the Three Sociologies, op. cit.* pp. 197–9.

47 For Engels' statements on the relationship between science and philosophy, see, in particular: *Anti-Dühring, op. cit.* Preface to 2nd edition 1885, pp. 17 and 20, and Introduction, pp. 35–6. See also 'Ludwig Feuerbach . . . ', *op. cit.*, p. 353. Even the very much earlier *German Ideology* presents a similar view: 'When reality is described, a self-sufficient philosophy loses its medium of existence. At the best its place can only to taken by a summing-up of the most general results, abstractions which are derived from the observation of the historical development of men'. (Marx and Engels, *Collected Works*, V (London 1976), p. 37)

48 Above, p. 15ff. Commentators are divided on the relation between Haeckel's thought and that of Engels. Timpanaro (*On Materialism, op. cit.* p. 88) argues that, a few remarks notwithstanding, Engels remained consistently a Darwinian rather than Lamarckian in his biological views. At the other extreme, Lichtheim (*Marxism* (London 1967), p. 244) argues that the evolution of Marxist thinking between the 1840s and 1880s can be summarized as: 'From Hegel to Haeckel'. That Lichtheim is mistaken is the main theme of the present section of this paper. Equally, though, Timpanaro's judgement cannot be sustained. The references he makes to Engels' critique of Haeckel

refer exclusively to Haeckels' social and philosophical thought, whilst
Engels consistently *follows* Haeckel on biological matters. Apart from
the references given elsewhere in this section of the paper, see *Anti-
Dühring*, pt. 1, ch. 7, where Engels uses Haeckel as an authority
alongside Darwin in defending a Haeckelian 'Darwinism' against
Dühring. *Anti-Dühring* p. 88, and *Dialectics of Nature*, p. 235, both
contain passages in which Engels supports Haeckelian, as against
Darwinian biological doctrines. In general, this evidence supports
the judgment of Gasman (*op. cit.*, p. 108ff.) that Engels followed
Haeckel on biological questions but had 'only contempt' for his social
and philosophical thought.

49 Above, p. 27.
50 Engels, *Anti-Dühring*, op. cit., p. 436.
51 Engels, *Dialectics of Nature*, op. cit., see, for example, p. 281.
52 See, for example, Marx's letter of 19 December 1860, quoted in
Gerratana (*op. cit.*) p. 63, and Marx's letter to F. Lassalle, 16 January
1861 (*Selected Correspondence*, *op. cit.*, p. 123), which are susceptible
of this interpretation. The very possibility of such a left-wing reductionism, though, illustrates the weakness of anti-reductionist critiques
of 'scientism', 'reification', etc., which equate political reaction with
reductionism. There is a tendency to this in, for example, the otherwise very valuable, 'Scientific racism and ideology', by S. Rose in
S. and H. Rose (eds.) *The Political Economy of Science* (London 1976),
pp. 112–41.
53 Marx's letter to Kugelmann, 27 June 187, Marx and Engels, *Selected
Correspondence*, op. cit., pp. 239–40.
54 S. Timpanaro, *On Materialism*, op. cit., p. 86.
55 There is evidence that Marx, too, was sceptical about the application
of Malthusian categories to organic nature (see Marx's letter to Engels,
18 June 1862, *Selected Correspondence*, p. 128). For Engels on this
question, see *Dialectic of Nature*, p. 208, and Engels' letter to Lavrov,
12–17 November 1875, in the *Selected Correspondence*, pp. 301–4.
See Gerratana, *New Left Review* 82, *op. cit.* p. 70ff., for an excellent
treatment of the inadequacy of Darwin's own view that natural
selection is Malthus applied to animals and plants.
56 Above, p. 8.
57 Engels, *Dialectics of Nature*, op. cit., p. 19.
58 Engels' Letter to Lange, 29 March 1865, *Selected Correspondence*,
op. cit., pp. 171–2.
59 Engels, *Dialectics of Nature*, op. cit., p. 19.
60 *Ibid*, p. 209.
61 *Ibid*, pp. 208–10, and *Selected Correspondence*, pp. 301–4.
62 Engels, *Dialectics of Nature*, op. cit., p. 209.
63 *Selected Correspondence*, p. 303.
64 Engels, *Dialectics of Nature*, op. cit., p. 19.
65 See above, note 65.
66 In this context, see Engels' letter to Lange (*Selected Correspondence*
p. 172) in which he tries to distinguish, among the laws and concepts

of political economy, those specific to bourgeois production and
distribution, and 'those which have hitherto been more or less valid
throughout all history'. A version of the foundation–superstructure
metaphor is used in 'Ludwig Feuerbach . . . ' to make a comparable
point about the relationships between the natural and social sciences
'For we live not only in nature but also in human society, and this
also no less than nature has its history of development and its science
It was therefore a question of bringing the science of society, that is
the sum total of the so-called historical and philosophical sciences
into harmony with the materialist foundation, and of reconstructing it
thereupon.' (*Selected Works*, XI, p. 340).

67   See above, p. 32 and note 52.

68   See, for example, Engels to Marx, 14 July 1858: ' . . . comparative
physiology gives one a withering contempt for the idealistic exaltation
of man over the other animals. At every step one bumps up against
the most complete uniformity of structure with the rest of the
mammals . . . The Hegelian business of the qualitative leap in the
quantitative series is also very fine here'. (*Selected Correspondence*
p. 109).

69   Examples include: H. Eysenck, *Race Intelligence and Education*
(London 1971); A. R. Jensen, *Educability and Group Differences*
(London 1973); Desmond Morris, *The Naked Ape* (London 1967) and
The Human Zoo (London 1969); E. O. Wilson, *Sociobiology : The
New Synthesis* (Cambridge, Mass 1975); and R. Ardrey, *The Territo-
rial Imperative* (London 1969)..

70   See P. Anderson, *Considerations on Western Marxism* (London 1976)
passim, for a wide-ranging discussion of the intellectual concerns
and orientations which makes this 'strategy' in relation to reactionary
appropriations of science intelligible. Even those Marxists who
have taken seriously the problem of critically confronting the cultural
effects of scientific knowledge have tended to one-sidedly engage in
critique of reactionary appropriations, to the neglect of the attempt to
achieve a progressive appropriation of scientific knowledge. For
example, the editorial collective of *Radical Science Journal* were able
to characterize their task in terms of 'attempting critiques of science
and technology' (*Radical Journal* (1978); p. 3).

71   I have in mind certain of the implications of the self-proclaimed
'rejection of epistemological discourse' by P. Q. Hirst and B. Hindess.
See, in particular, their *Mode of Production and Social Formation*
(London 1977), pp. 6–8 and ch. 1. See *Radical Philosophy* XX, 1978
for critiques of the idealism in this position by A. Collier, and A. Skil-
len, and the extended version of Collier's paper in the present volume

5 *Historical Materialism*

GEOFFREY HELLMAN

Introduction

IN the course of his break with Hegelian idealism, Marx
developed an orientation toward society and history which he
believed opened the way to a new social science capable of
abstracting social wholes and their parts in a way that would
allow formulation of lawful relationships while at the same
time demystifying the phenomena of alienation – the domination of humans by their productions – and illuminating the
role of political and legal forms and what he called 'forms of
consciousness'. However, no more than a few pages were
devoted by Marx to the explicit formulation of principles
underlying this orientation, principles forming the core of
'historical materialism'. Fundamental to this approach is the
division of social systems into a material base, or mode of
production, and a superstructure[1] along with the claim that
'the mode of production in material life determines [*bedingen*]
the general character of the social, political, and spiritual
processes of life'.[2] Unfortunately, since these few pages,
little real progress has been made in developing the substantive theory of historical materialism.[3] My aim in this paper is
to carry inquiry a step further by first setting forth some
minimal conditions of adequacy that principles of historical
materialism should meet and then developing two types of
principles, compatible with the criteria, relating the material
base and superstructure of social systems, which seem to lead
in the most promising direction. However, while I believe that
the principles to be presented are, in motivation, amply
supported by Marx's corpus and also by Engels' historical
writing,[4] my concern is with the principles and not with
textual authority for them.

  These principles concern the general problem of assigning
a priority to one part of an evolving complex system whose

parts are all to some extent interdependent. Thus, in addition to their relevance for social theory, the principles to be presented are potentially of interest to other sciences dealing with evolving complex systems (such as biology and ecology) and to those concerned to develop a general theory of complex systems.

The first type of principle depends on the notion of 'conflict' or 'incompatibility' within a system, which is construed in purely causal terms. The second depends on the idea of assigning different weights to various causal factors involved in producing change within a system; the notion of weighting is analysed in terms presupposing the existence of certain causal laws governing change in social systems, with minimal assumptions as to the applicability of quantitative analysis. An intuitive argument is then presented to the effect that, for many systems, the two principles are equivalent. The conclusion is thereby supported that historical materialism has a coherent and substantial formulation that does justice to the complexity of social phenomena.

Before proceeding, it would be well to answer an objection sometimes raised (especially by Marxists) against trying to formulate general principles relating base and superstructure. It runs thus:

> One of historical materialism's greatest insights was that 'economic laws' are historically specific to a particular mode of production and cannot be framed ahistorically in terms of the species' relation to nature. If this is true in the sphere of production itself, should it not be expected to hold with respect to the relations between the sphere of production and the superstructure?[5]

It is true that Marx was wary about generalizing on such matters; and examples such as Lukacs' to the effect that primitive art relates to its material base differently from, say, art under capitalism must be taken seriously.[6] Such examples, however, only show that general principles are apt to be more complex, at least in their applications, than might have been expected; they do not show there are no general principles. Nor did Marx prove there are no transhistorical laws meriting the title 'economic'. Rather he argued that the salient phenomena that classical political economy needed to explain (crises of overproduction, for example) were to be accounted for in terms specific to the capitalist mode of production and were not manifestations of laws relating the species directly to nature. Moreover, the categories, 'mode of production', 'superstructure', 'ideology', 'forms of conscious-ness', etc., are in fact applicable to a wide variety of societies, in contrast to the 'specific' terms of political economy ('exchange value', 'capital', and so forth). In so far, generaliza-tion across different types of social systems interrelating these categories is not open to the kind of specificity objections that apply to political economy. Furthermore, the principles to be set forth are confined to spelling out 'the primacy of material conditions' in human social life. These by no means exhaust historical materialism but are rather core principles to which more specific ones must be added in a developed theory. Ultimately an account should be provided as to the way more special relations between base and superstructure (and among their components) depend on their changing content. If, however, there are *no* general claims as to the primacy of material conditions, historical materialism cannot claim even to provide a general framework for social and historical explanation. It is hard, in that case, to see what a materialist worthy of the name could appeal to in accounting for why the 'primacy of material conditions' is restricted.

The Material Base

A great many confusions and pitfalls can be avoided if, at the outset, some fundamental points are clarified concerning the nature of the material base of a social system.[7]

I am taking the material base to be the same as the material mode of production where this is understood to comprise what Marx calls the social forces of production and the social relations of production. Sometimes only the social relations are included directly, but the forces then enter indirectly since relations of production include relations of power and control over the various forces of production.

First, it is to be stressed that neither forces nor relations of production have exclusively to do with technology. This is trivial with respect to relations of production, but is true also with respect to forces, since these include aspects of organization of the work process – especially facts concerning the division of labour – directly related to the social productivity of labour. Historical meterialism is not intended to be any form of technological determinism. *Social relations of production include relations of domination, subordination, and control among humans in the work process and between human and non-human productive forces.* However important technology may be, it is evident that widely different patterns of real power relations in the work process can coexist with a given technology, and moreover that the direction in the development of technology is itself in large measure governed by relations of power and social class interests in the work process.

Second, however, social relations of production are distinct from legal rights. Though they often coincide, they frequently do not. From the point of view of materialism, legal systems and codes are grounded in relations of social power in the process of production, and their development is guided thereby.[8]

Finally, a point too seldom emphasized, it is obvious, given our definition of 'relations of production', that elements of 'consciousness' embracing a wide range of higher-order cognitive and psychological activity – perception, belief, desire, decision making, emotions etc. – are to some extent included in the base, since they are part and parcel of. relations of power and control. Confusion arises partly because Marx and Marxists frequently speak of 'forms of consciousness' as belonging to the superstructure; and there is the famous encapsulation from the 'Preface': 'It is not the consciousness of humans that determines their existence, but, on the contrary, their social existence determines their consciousness.'[9] But this *is* no more than an encapsulation of a previous passage to the effect that the mode of production determines the general character of forms of social consciousness. This by no means restricts the psychological component of the base to matters on the order of the reflex arc! The distinction wanted is between, on the one hand, forms of social consciousness – ideologies, codes of conduct, and promulgated doctrine concerned with the justification of general social arrangements, frequently the province of special institutions (for example churches, schools) – and, on the other, beliefs expectations, and other dispositions to decision and action which are either prerequisite to or directly part of carrying out day-to-day functions in the work process. Although the former affect the exercize of power in the work process and although the line separating the two is sometimes hard to draw, the distinction is real and important. To deny it would be to deny, for example, that it is meaningful to speak of a wage system under capitalism, or a 'market in labour', or a great many totalities of the sort that social theorists and economists of all schools recognize, and recognize to be distinct from typical components of the superstructure. For it would not be possible to describe, say, the operation of the wage system in any historical situation without reference to such psychological factors as investment decisions by capitalists, dispositions of workers to enter into a contract with employers, their realization that unemployed compete for limited employment, and so forth. Moreover, religious doctrine, say, may influence the wage system but is not part of it. This does not imply that each psychological factor which is included in a particular wage system at a time is essential to the wage system described at a general level in social theory. Indeed, at the level of general theory, a great many specifics are 'accidental', including membership by particular individuals in social classes. (This helps account for the tendency to think of psychological specifics as not part of totalities such as the wage system.) Specification of particulars enters when the theory is applied to a particular system at a time, much as the values of state variables for a physical system get specified only in applications of physical theory. What interesting generalizations exist at the social theoretic level concerning the psychological component of the material base is thus an entirely distinct question, beyond the scope of this paper.

Adequacy Conditions and Some Violations
In order to guide investigation and at the same time highlight the inadequacy of certain common formulations, some minimal conditions of adequacy on historical materialist principles will be useful.

Let us use b to range over base conditions (or variables)

and s for superstructural conditions (or variables), and let us use the neutral term 'element' to refer to components of either that would be recognized by a developed theory of social systems (including events, processes, states, and other complex objects such as practices or institutions). Now one assumption generally recognized by materialists is a *Principle of Interdependence*:

> For most historically significant elements x of either b or s, laws of x's time development depend on both b and s, that is, require antecedent conditions on variables from both b and s.

Thus, neither the base nor the superstructure (nor any significant parts thereof) is seen as developing in isolation. This is reasonable on empirical grounds and recognizes the complexity of the systems under investigation. In accordance with this, the first adequacy condition may be framed thus:

(1) Principles of historical materialism must be compatible with the Principle of Interdependence; they must not imply that the material base uniquely determines the super-structure.[10]

This should be adopted on empirical grounds. Although it may not be possible to observe two actual systems exactly alike in all relevant base respects, the prospect of unique determination of systems as complex as social systems by even so rich a part as the material base is too much to expect.[11]

The second adequacy condition is as follows:

(2) Principles spelling out historical materialism must not be truistic; moreover, they must not be ultimately metaphorical or vague; specifically, any occurrences of phrases such as 'more important' or its cognates must be clarified and ultimately replaced.

Thus, according to (2), historical materialism must be claiming more than that material conditions contribute to the formation and content of the superstructure; and it is not enough to say, without further analysis, that the base plays a more important causal role in producing x (whatever x is focussed upon) than the superstructure. (2) is stated in the interests of scientific progress and with the conviction that disputes between materialists and their opponents over the nature of society and history are non-trivial.

Thirdly, we require:

(3) Principles of historical materialism must not be *invertible*, in the following sense: they must provide that it is not arbitrary that the base is construed as a 'real foundation' and the superstructure as 'an edifice arising on the foundation';[12] it must not be equally valid to turn the picture upside down. More precisely, a principle of historical materialism, if empirically confirmed (or if true or otherwise justified), must not be transformable to an equally confirmed (true, or justified) principle upon systematic permutation of the terms 'base' and 'superstructure' with each other.

Thus, any principle to the effect that it is necessary to take account of relations to base elements in assessing the role of (say) some superstructural element will not meet condition (3) because it would be just as valid to say that it is necessary to take account of relations to superstructural elements in assessing the role of some base element.

This non-invertibility requirement is frequently overlooked in discussions of historical materialism, and its satisfaction proves difficult to establish once the first two requirements are met. (Principles claiming 'greater importance' for the base are trivially non-invertible but violate condition (2).) Before leaving this section, it will be instructive to consider how (3) operates to rule out as insufficient an otherwise promising effort.

For example, consider a natural weakening of unique determination by the base (ruled out by (1)), which might be called 'loose determination': in any two (scientifically possible) systems which are identical (up to isomorphism) on their base elements at a time, difference among their s elements are restricted to a narrow range of alternatives at that time (compared with the total range of variation compatible, say, with various sets of exogenous conditions). While reasonable, it is not necessary to go further to see that it is invertible, violating (3). For it is equally the case that the superstructure loosely determines the base (*mutatis mutandis*). In fact, the latter 'loose determination' may be even tighter than the former: given a description of legal and political forms, ideologies, artistic styles, etc., one may be in an even better position to reconstruct the productive forces and relations than *vice versa*. In short, the inference from different *b* to different *s* may be better supported than the converse, from same *b* to same *s*. Thus, such a principle cannot serve as a formulation of historical materialism.

The problem with loose determination is that it is static: it relies implicitly on a notion of 'compatibility' between *b* and *s* elements at a time without saying anything about the development of the system over time. Likewise, it says nothing about the causal production of elements of the system. Consideration of dynamical principles is in order.

Compatibility and Survival
One sort of dynamical principle that has been proposed is based on an analogy with evolution through natural selection in biology. As motivation, consider ideology. At any time, there may be arising – randomly, from the standpoint of social theory – a wide variety of ideas on some major issue such as the justification of political authority, the source of order in the universe, and so forth. Yet a definite current of thought on any such matter is predominant, or else a small number of currents are vying with one another. Other views either die out or survive without having any impact (or do not arise at all). Social theory should explain this phenomenon of selection for survival and effectiveness. Historical materialism attempts to provide a general pattern for such explanation. It claims that survival and effectiveness of *s* elements are based on class interests, which are in turn spelled out in terms of production relations, the interests of the classes dominant in the mode of production taking precedence over others in the selection process. In its barest form, this may be stated thus:

(4) An *s* element in a social system *S*, in order to survive

and be historically effective, must be compatible with the prevailing mode of production or material base.

As it stands, of course, this is very vague.[13] An important task is to spell out and interrelate the complex notions of 'survival', 'effectiveness', and 'compatibility'. The question I wish to focus on is whether (4) meets the non-invertibility requirement.

(4) treats the base as an environment in which various s elements compete for survival over time. It is not obvious, however, that the analogy is not invertible. For why is it not the case that at a given time, the superstructure constitutes an environment selecting out b alternatives competing with each other for survival and effectiveness? One can give examples lending support to this inverted principle. (For example, prevailing political opinion 'selecting out' one production technique over others, depending on, say, the expected resulting unemployment.) Perhaps natural selection in a relatively stable background environment is the wrong model, a better one being an ecosystem consisting of a pair of relatively symbiotic species, each of which counts equally as part of the environment for the other. If so, it would seem that the non-invertibility requirement cannot be met, and that historical materialism could not claim more than to have discovered one important set of lawful connections between what it had quite arbitrarily called the 'real foundation' of social systems and the 'edifice arising upon the foundation'.

Isolated examples of the superstructure acting as an environment with respect to base alternatives do not show that base and superstructure are on a par. Materialism need not deny that in some cases the superstructure acts as an environment; it is sufficient to claim that social systems are substantially weighted toward the base insofar as the environment-selection model is concerned. One way of capturing this is to consider patterns of resolution of various sorts of conflicts or incompatibilities in a social system.

But what is an 'incompatibility' and how precisely can such a notion be used in formulating principles that improve upon (4)? The remainder of this section will be devoted to sketching an explication of this notion of 'incompatibility' and introducing a closely related notion, that of one part of a system 'yielding' to another part, and then using these ideas to formulate a principle in the spirit of the environment-selection model that meets the non-invertibility and other requirements already introduced. One of our aims here is to suggest how this may be done in a way that essentially demystifies notions such as 'incompatibility' and 'contradiction' and brings principles that employ such ideas within the overall framework of the natural sciences.

In accordance with this, one employs the notion of a 'scientific law', or 'true, lawlike generalization', as this term is used in current discussions in the philosophy of science. Although there is to date no generally accepted explication of this notion, there is widespread agreement that the distinction marked between a lawful and an accidental generalization is important and in some measure objectively grounded (though certain conventional and anthropocentric aspects do not seem entirely eliminable). The generally recognized mark of a lawlike sentence (we restrict attention to universal conditional sentences of the form 'All F are G') is that, in contrast to accidental sentences, it supports counterfactual assertions of the form, 'if x had been F, it would have been (or become) G'. Thus, a sentence such as 'all ruling classes attempt to maintain their dominant position' might qualify as lawlike whereas 'all ruling classes consist of persons in the highest income tenth' would probably not qualify. A further widely recognized point is that lawlikeness depends critically on the character of the predicates (general descriptive terms) entering into the statement of a law. Such predicates must individuate and classify entities in appropriate ways in order to enter into lawlike sentences. (Again, just what conditions such predicates or 'natural kind terms' must meet is a controversial matter.) Some have argued that higher level disciplines such as psychology and the social sciences do not contain any laws because their vocabularies are inappropriate. Without entering into this, I am proceeding on the view that many of the predicates of historically materialist oriented social science do divide the social world into 'kinds of entities' such that, at least in principle, approximately true lawlike generalizations are forthcoming. (Predicates classifying people according to their roles in processes of production would be important examples here.) Before proceeding, a few remarks on this assumption are in order.

Owing to the complexity of social systems, few if any exact general laws are known governing the behaviour of such systems. In practice, a lawlike relationship is indicated by forming a truncated statement that omits mention of many variables, relies heavily on a *ceteris paribus* clause, and perhaps refers to 'tendencies', 'increased likelihoods', and so forth. Genuine laws would not contain such amorphous terminology (though one may want to admit statistical statements as laws). In principle, formulation of exact genuine laws for social systems may not be possible without an extensive, new technical vocabulary. One is assuming, however (with the use of the term 'approximately' above), that such a vocabulary would contain terms that are a *refinement* of the existing vocabulary. Further, one recognizes that elimination of *ceteris paribus* clauses very likely would involve introducing predicates for factors outside the domain of social science proper, as currently understood (for example factors from the biological sciences that play a role in determination of human behaviour). This further highlights how far away from exact general laws one is in practice. The claim that, say, Marxian social theoretic vocabulary is appropriate for the formulation in principle (quite apart from the discovery) of genuine laws (even approximately true laws) is thus a rather strong claim. Some might in fact wish to call this a, or even *the*, principle of historical materialism. One agrees that such a claim is part of historical materialism, but it is essentially weaker than the principles sketched below. This is because the 'lawlike character' of historical materialist vocabulary is quite compatible with there being no real primacy of material conditions in history. On the present view, one must go further and say something about the content of these idealized laws into which this vocabulary may enter.

To proceed with the proposal, let us introduce the notion of an element x of a social system S *surviving over* another element y in a given time period (say, from t to t') to mean: x continues to exist in S from t to t' and y either alters substantially or ceases to exist by t'. This is a non-modal relation that obtains between many elements that may not be causally connected in any interesting way. (For example, a certain legal practice may survive over an artistic style in a particular period in a given system, although the passing of the latter may be adequately accounted for without reference to the persisting legal practice.) Nevertheless, if one allows such a relation to enter into the formulation of scientific laws, and it is assumed that such laws do express causal dependencies, then one can combine these notions to explicate 'incompatibility' as follows:

> Elements x and y in system S are incompatible (in period t-t')
> iff
> there exists a scientific law which takes an antecedent condition describing the state of S with x and y at t to the consequent condition that 'either x survives over y or y survives over x in the period t-t''.

For this to make sense, it must be presupposed that an appropriate notion of 'state of the system' is forthcoming. This amounts to the assumption that social systems and their components have been classified and described in a scientific vocabulary that 'isolates' relevant causal variables or properties (qualtitative as well as quantitative). As in the natural sciences, such a process goes hand in hand with the process of formulating laws; thus, this assumption is subsumed under one that has already been made, that dynamical laws of at least an approximate character are in principle forthcoming for social systems. (Nothing in these assumptions should be taken to imply, however, that there is a unique vocabulary for framing such laws.) Given all this, incompatible elements (relative to a time period) are those that 'cannot' persist together throughout that period in the sense that some causal mechanism requires the elimination or substantial alteration of one of the elements.[14] (The reader may well ask, what about cases where conflicting elements both alter or disappear? This important class of cases has been omitted only in order to simplify the discussion. It should be clear that the definitions can be amended to cover such cases.)

While keeping track of the assumptions, it should be mentioned that the above notion of incompatibility contains a special element of vagueness in the reference to 'substantial alteration' of an element. This, however, need not be seen as violating the spirit of the second adequacy condition, since there is a large measure of agreement between materialists and their opponents as to what counts here in particular contexts. The same may be said for certain further points of glaring vagueness shortly to appear.

It might be thought that an appropriate historical materialist principle would be simply that a numerical preponderance of cases of incompatibility between actual base and superstructural elements are resolved in favour of the base. This, however, leaves out of account the important phenomenon of part of a system preventing elements from arising in another part. For example, a dominant set of property relations may function so as to rule out in advance certain social or political practices that *would* result in an incompatibility *were* they to arise. To omit such considerations would be seriously to underestimate the extent to which existing arrangements constrain alternatives that otherwise could arise and have an historical impact. What one needs to do, then, is extend the notion of incompatibility to cover such cases.

There is a danger here of lapsing into nonsense in attempting to describe relations between actual and 'merely possible' elements. Instead of such talk, one may appeal to *descriptions* of 'possible elements' in an adequate theoretical vocabulary. That is, one may speak of various *kinds* of events, practices, etc: (corresponding to predicates of the presupposed scientific language) having no instances at a given time in a given system due to the operation of laws of the sort one has been considering. Such laws may take the form: 'Any system S (of the appropriate type) whose base (respectively, superstructure) satisfies conditions $C_1 \ldots C_n$ at time t will not exhibit any superstructural (respectively, base) element of kind K in the neighbourhood of t.' Here, the C_1 describe relevant aspects of the state of part of S at t and K describes a kind of element that is 'blocked' or 'prevented from arising' in the other part.[15] In case such a law obtains, one may speak of the existing base (or superstructure) as incompatible with 'elements of kind K'. Thus there are two types of incompatibilities: one between actual elements that get resolved by the survival of one over the other (in which case one may say 'adaptation' to the surviving element has occurred); and a second between an existing part of a system and kinds of 'possible elements' blocked by the existing part. Let us cover these two types of phenomena with a single term by saying that *y yields to x* if and only if either x and y are incompatible in the first sense (y and x are existing elements) and x survives over y according to law, or x and y are incompatible in the second sense (that is y is a relevant kind of alternative 'possible element') and x blocks y. (Both sides of this definition should be relativized to time intervals.)

Now *yields* yields a principle of the sort one has been seeking. To state it, it is convenient to subdivide the incompatibilities (in the general sense just introduced) into two categories (based now on the parts of the system between which they obtain): Category I consists of incompatibilities between existing s and b elements and between kinds of s alternatives and b; category II consists of incompatibilities between kinds of b alternatives and existing s. The principle runs thus:

(5) In systems S developing over time the following obtains:
    (a) In a large preponderance of category I incompatibilities, the s element or kind of alternative yields to the base;
    (b) In a relatively small proportion of category II incompatibilities, the b kind of alternative yields to the superstructure.

Because of the central role of the notion of conflict, this may be called 'dialectical base predominance'. It says that, while fixing either part of a system restricts the other part, the restriction on b from fixing s is not as severe as the reverse, not in the sense of what is compatible at a time (the notion relevant to 'loose determination', see above, the second section), but rather in the sense of how conflicts are or would be resolved over time. In other words (5) implies that *s* adapts to *b* far more readily than *b* adapts to *s* and *b* blocks *s* alternatives far more readily than *s* blocks *b* alternatives.

Obviously, (5) is non-invertible and compatible with the Principle of Interdependence. Equally obviously, it is impossible at this level of generality to be precise as to the difference in the proportions referred to. However, since materialists will surely not be satisfied with small differences here, there is no obstacle in principle to developing more precise standards for particular applications which both materialists and their opponents would recognize.[16] Further, (5) can serve as a guide in developing more refined hypotheses dealing with specific types of incompatibilities.

In considering (5), only serious incompatibilities having historically significant consequences are relevant in making the comparisons called for. What counts as serious depends in part on a framework of inquiry and the purposes and interests of theory construction. All principles of historical materialism are affected at certain points by the problem of *selection* confronting social theory generally, the problem of deciding what is worth accounting for and what is not. However, vagueness on this point does not vitiate principles such as (5) because, to the extent that there is real disagreement between materialists and non-materialists over the nature of social change, there must be a significant area of prior agreement over what phenomena merit explanation. Otherwise all disagreement would be located at the level of selection and not at the level of lawful relationships. While indeed the area of agreement in selection is very far from total, it is, one assumes, sufficient to support a real debate as to the sorts of laws that govern social change.[17]

This is not the place to argue the truth of (5). Rather the task is to formulate principles conforming to the adequacy conditions and to make clear their plausibility and coherence. It is worth noting, however, that some widely recognized social phenomena lend credibility to Dialectical Base Predominance. One is the phenomenon of superstructural transformation in periods of revolutions in production relations in which base transformations are preserved and reinforced by those transformations. Another is that of 'cultural lag', in which ideas and attitudes outmoded by base changes persist without blocking or undermining those changes, ultimately giving way to new cultural expessions. Such phenomena, along with many others one can cite, support a significant difference in weighting between base and superstructure, and suggest that the selection model of (4) does not readily apply in inverted form (with s as environment) due to prevailing patterns of conflict resolution in favour of the material base. This difference in weighting can also be approached from another route, which may now be elucidated.

Differential Predominance

For motivation, it is helpful to recall the historical context of historical materialism as Marx and Engels developed it. That was the growing strength and cohesiveness of the European working classes and the challenge this presented to capital. Historical materialism was conceived as an approach to the political task that appeared on the historical agenda: the emancipation of labour. As such it was counterposed primarily to reformism, on the one hand, and utopianism on the other. In sum, it said that such changes in production relations as would constitute labour's emancipation could come neither through manipulating the existing political and legal institutions nor through the promulgation of utopian blueprints for a 'better society'. The major source for such changes was seen to be within the base itself, in the growing crises of the capitalist system combined with the direct struggle by labour itself (*not* any self-proclaimed 'representatives') for control over the means of production.

Underlying this is the view that production relations are far less susceptible to large-scale change 'from above', from the prevailing superstructure, than they are 'from below', from within the base itself. It is important to note that the point is comparative; the Principle of Interdependence is not in question. Thus, the crucial notion to be analysed is that of differential susceptibility to change from different parts of a system, all of which, by hypothesis, make some contribution to the change in question.

The problem may be posed abstractly means of a diagram:

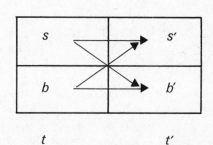

Here, S is a social system enduring through a time period divided into two parts indicated by t and t' (t' later than t), and S is divided into the two tiers at each period. The arrows from left to right indicate, intuitively, the contribution of factors within the left sector to the production of a change at the level represented by the arrow's head. What is called for is a comparison in relative weighting between various arrows: at a minimum, in accordance with the above motivation, it is necessary to explicate 'bb' has greater weight than sb'' (abbreviated '$bb' > sb'$'). How can this be done?

One way would be as follows: let r' represent the statement that a significant change in a single base variable, r, has occurred in S from t to t' (for example r' might say that in a capitalist system unemployment has risen by more than some amount). Let $C_1^b \ldots C_n^b$ represent antecedent base conditions in the time period t and let $C_1^s \ldots C_m^s$ represent antecedent superstructural conditions in that period such that there is a lawlike truth of the form:

(6) If C_0 and C_1^b and ... and C_n^b and C_1^s and ... and C_m^s, then r'

where C_0 represents other initial conditions (concerning the environment of S at t) required to get the result r'. (Perhaps, also, it is necessary to add a probability value in the consequent, so that (6) would say that given the antecedent conditions on S at t, r' at t' is probable to degree p. For simplicity, I will suppress mention of probabilities.) Thus, in our example, the C_1^b might be conditions causing a fall in the rate of profit along with capitalists' dispositions to maximize profits, to save, etc.; the C_1^s might be conditions regarding government policy, beliefs in the moral and property rights of capitalists, etc.; and C_0 might concern exogenous factors such as the absence of world war, and so forth.

Now it may be supposed that none of the antecedent conditions in a law of form (6) is superfluous; that is, varying any one of them while holding the rest fixed would alter the value of r. But this does not mean that all the antecedent conditions are on a par. It may be, for instance, that the total change in r that would theoretically follow upon varying any or all of the C_1^b while holding the C_1^s and C_0 fixed would far exceed that which would follow upon varying any or all of the C_1^s while holding C_1^b and C_0 fixed. The variable r could then be said to be more *susceptible to change from* b *than to change from* s. I shall refer to this method as the *differential method*.[18] It will be further elaborated shortly. With its aid, the general weighting claim at issue can be defined:

(7) $bb' > sb'$ iff

a preponderance of b variables, v_b, at most times are more susceptible to change from b than to change from s, according to the differential method applied to laws of from (6) with the v_b as resultant.

A major assumption behind the differential method is that causal laws of form (6) govern social systems. Nothing, however, is assumed as to methods of discovering such laws, a distinct question that will not be considered here. Important as it is, the problem of discovery need not be solved in order to give a coherent formulation of historical materialism. The differential method is thus to be contrasted with Mill's method of differences, explicitly a canon of discovery which, moreover, Mill thought inapplicable to the social sciences due to absence of experimental control. Suffice it to say that scientific discovery is recognized to be far more complex than Mill supposed, and the absence of laboratory control by no means dictates indiscoverability of the kinds of relationships to which the differential method pertains.[19]

Two further problems arising in connection with the

differential method merit attention. First, there is what may be called the problem of interdependence: since the b and the s of a system are not isolated from each other, it is generally not possible to vary conditions in one domain while holding those in the other fixed. Of course, absolute fixity is not required; approximate fixity (according to appropriate natural metrics for the conditions in question if they can be found) would suffice. Furthermore, as noted in the previous section, the vocabulary entering into the laws may be quite technical and refined compared with current history writing. Materialism presupposes that relatively independent b and s variables are in principle isolable, not that one can now give a precise list. This sense of independent variability of a set of variables – that some can in theory be varied while others remain fixed – is, of course, entirely compatible with the Principle of Interdependence.[20] Finally, I claim that the search for independent variability will help guide the development of scientific language here as it has elsewhere.

Counter to this is what may be called the doctrine of *strict organicity*. According to it, social systems are so throughly interdependent that independently varying variables are not isolable in principle. Roughly, significant variation of any part of the system, regardless of how it is abstracted, is incompatible with even approximate fixity of any other part. Strict organicity, unlike the Principle of Interdependence, thus implies that the differential method is inapplicable to these systems, either for purposes of discovering laws of form (6) or for theoretically clarifying causal weighting. It is probably the case that, since historical materialism assigns causal priority to the material base and thereby requires something like the differential method, strict organicity is incompatible with historical materialism.

Briefly, three points can be made against strict organicity. (1) A great many causal connections that can already be drawn in our undeveloped vocabulary belie it. (Consider the falling profit-rising unemployment example above: quite clearly, reducing the rate of profit need not alter all other antecedent conditions, such as attitudes concerning property rights.) (2) Considerations of the evolution of complex systems, biological as well as social, point strongly against their strict-organic character in favour of a property of near-decomposability into relatively stable sub-systems.[21] (3) The solar system is organic in the sense that one could not alter one part without in some degree affecting the others; yet differential methods can be applied to predict the motions of the parts to within remarkable limits of accuracy. What strict organicism ignores is that much abstraction and idealization go into formulating scientific laws, and part of the success of this process is that it allows theoretical variation of some of the properties abstracted without upsetting the whole enterprise. Seen in this light, strict organicism appears as a form of scepticism with little foundation other than current ignorance.

Now to the second problem with the differential method, the problem of measurement. An adequate treatment of this difficult matter is beyond the scope of this paper. What can be done here is to raise the issue and to indicate how, at least in favourable cases, it may be approached.

The task is to make sense of claims like (7), which appeal to laws of form (6) treating a single resultant at a time. As already indicated (See note 18), working with laws of this form rather than more general laws describing the total resultant state of the system has the advantage of minimizing problems of heterogeneity: if the resultant r is a complex of several variables (say, x, y, z), then in order for the differential method to apply, there must be standards for comparing different changes in r corresponding to different changes in the x, y, z components. Suppose, for instance, that on holding s antecedent conditions nearly fixed while varying b conditions, one gets a doubling of the quantity x while y and z increase only slightly, whereas on holding b fixed while varying s one gets an increase of 66 percent in each of x, y, and z. Is one to count these changes as equal or unequal, and if unequal, which is greater? Without decisions as to relative weighting of the components there is no determinate answer. In some cases, there may be clear grounds for a particular assignment of weights, but in general many different choices will appear equally valid. By focussing on laws of form (6), where the consequent involves a single magnitude r, this problem of weighting is replaced by the problem of selecting historically significant resultants together with the problem of deciding what is to count as a 'preponderance' of such resultants. Here again mere counting of magnitudes is bound to be simplistic, and decisions comparing different sets of changes (based now on a set of different laws of form (6)) will be called for. In effect, then, one problem of weighting has been replaced by another, but one that enters at a later stage in the comparisons.

Here the best course would seem to be to construe claims like (7) as asserting that the 'preponderance' predicted will be clear enough so as to be unaffected by any delicate weighting considerations. The selection of relevant resultants r must be based on prior agreement on what is to be explained, and, further, the predictions of the materialist must be that susceptibility to change from the base markedly outweighs that from the superstructure in a significant majority of cases to which the theory is designed to apply.[22] To avoid circularity, of course, the materialist must be prepared to specify in advance what these cases are. In particular contexts, there does not appear to be any insurmountable obstacle to doing this.

So far, then, some sense has been made of the claim that the arrow $bb' > sb'$.[23] This, however, is not a sufficient claim for historical materialism, because nothing has yet been said as to its invertibility. If the inverted claim, $ss' > bs'$, were equally supportable, the upshot would be a relative autonomy of the two domains, each playing the greater role in its own evolution.

It may be asked, why not compare the diagonals, bs' and sb', from the diagram? The claim that $bs' > sb'$, if true, is not invertible. The foundational character of the base would then consist in its putting greater 'pressure' on the superstructure than the latter puts on it. The trouble with this is that the differential method does not readily apply to comparisons of arrows with heads in different domains. As long as both heads are in the same domain, a comparison can be made by consulting sufficiently many laws of from (6) with appropriately chosen r from that domain. (Of course, approximate equality is a possible outcome.) But when the heads are in different domains, the differential method would work only if the resultants were selected as complexes with components from both b and s. Here, as already mentioned, serious problems of heterogeneity arise, since it would be necessary to have a single metric for changes in the complex factor based on changes in the components. Direct comparison of the diagonals seems a will-o-the-wisp.

In addition to the claim that $bb' > sb'$, materialism can simply maintain the negation of $ss' > bs'$, that is of the claim that a preponderance of r in s are more susceptible to differential variation of s conditions than to such variation of b conditions. At least materialism must claim that the base plays as great a role in the development of s as s does. On the whole, this is plausible. In stable periods, s may have a good deal of autonomy, whereas in periods of transformation, new foundations are laid for new superstructural elements with the base playing the predominant role. Further refinements along these lines require investigation. At this point, one has:

(8) In systems S diagrammed into the two tiers over time:
    (a) $bb' > sb'$ and
    (b) it is not the case that $ss' > bs'$.

Depending on how the selection problem is resolved, clause (b) could be strengthened. In particular, if attention is focused on major social transformations in which new classes come to power and old ones die out, then the stronger claim,

(8′) In systems S diagrammed into two tiers over time:
    (a) $bb' > sb'$ and
    (b) $bs' > ss'$

would be appropriate. These may be called principles of *Differential Base Predominance*.

What is the relationship between Differential Base Predominance and Dialectical Base Predominance? Although they are logically independent, an intuitive argument can be given that, for a wide class of systems satisfying some further conditions, the two principles coincide. It must be assumed that the various proportions referred to in the two types of principles are taken to be roughly the same in the corresponding clauses ((a) and (b), respectively). Clause (b) of (5) could be given a weak reading (so that the complement of a small proportion need not be a 'preponderance'), in which case the relevant comparison is with (8). On its more natural strong reading, the comparison is with (8′).

To illustrate the general relationship, consider the direction from Differential Base Predominance (8′) to Dialectical Base Predominance. Suppose that in a system S the latter fails, specifically, clause (a) of (5) fails. Then in a sizeable proportion (whose complement is no preponderance) of conflicts between some b element x and existing s or s alternatives y,y does not yield to b. But, since these are cases of incompatibility, x must yield to the s elements, y. Thus, a change in b is or would be produced by s elements, despite any tendency from within b to preserve x. It is plausible that such b elements x are more susceptible to change from within s than from within b. Provided such cases of conflict between b and s are a representative sample of the totality of relevant causal interactions between b and s, it would follow that $bb′ \not> sb′$, contradicting (a) of (8′). If (5) fails due to clause (b), a parallel argument can be made for failure of clause (b) of (8′). In both cases, the key assumptions are (i) that weakness in the tendency of elements z in a domain to preserve a compatible element x of the same domain corresponds to a pattern of relatively small change in x on varying z while holding other antecedent conditions (in laws of form (6)) fixed; and (ii) that the conflict cases form a representative sample of the relevant causal interactions. That these conditions obtain would seem a reasonable working hypothesis. To get an equally convincing (and messy) argument from (5) to (8′), just reverse the steps in the above.

It is by no means claimed that these principles exhaust the important relations historical materialism may claim to hold between base and superstructure. In particular, it is an interesting and open question whether the dependence there may be of symbolic content of art and other symbolic activity upon material conditions can adequately be treated as a special case of Dialectical Base Predominance or Differential Base Predominance. The delineation of these principles and their approximate convergence do support within certain limits of vagueness especially concerning problems of selection and measurement, the view that a core of historical materialism has a coherent, non-trivial formulation, compatible with the full complexity of social systems actually observed while at the same time giving the material base a truly foundational role in the development and transformation of the social world.

Notes

1 The material base is taken to comprise forces and relations of production and is discussed in the first section. The superstructure includes political and legal institutions, legal, religious, and moral codes, belief systems concerning the justification of social arrangements (ideologies), scientific and philosophic systems of thought, and the arts. Obviously the superstructure of any social system is highly complex, and some of its parts are more tightly connected to the material base than others. Below, I abstract from this complexity in the belief that (1) the division between base and superstructure is more fundamental than other divisions, especially from the standpoint of the large-scale historical transformations of social systems; and (2) clarity on the relationship between base and superstructure is indispensable for further investigation of the interrelations among other parts of such systems.

2 Karl Marx, 'Preface' to *A Contribution to the Critique of Political Economy*, in *Karl Marx: The Essential Writings*, F. J. Bender (ed.) (New York 1972), pp. 161f.

3 For a recent exception, in my estimation, see J. McMurtry, 'Making sense of economic determinism', *Canadian Journal of Philosophy*, III, ch. 2 (Dec. 1973), pp. 249–61.

4 For an especially good example, see Friedrich Engels, *Germany: Revolution and Counter-revolution*, Leonard Krieger (ed.) (Chicago 1967).

5 This paraphrases a view of G. Lukacs in 'The changing function of historical materialism', in *History and Class Consciousness* (Cambridge, Mass. 1971), pp. 223–55. On specificity, see Karl Korsch, *Three Essays on Marxism* (London 1971), ch. 1.

6 G. Lukacs, *op. cit.*, 236.

7 The first two points below are also made by McMurtry, *op. cit.* They are frequently enough misunderstood to bear repetition.

8 The point has been made by Gerald A. Cohen, 'On some criticisms of historical materialism', *The Aristotelian Society Supplement*, XLIV (1970), 121–41.

9 Karl Marx, *loc. cit.*

10 Unique determination has two interpretations, a static one and a dynamic one. Statically, part P of a system S determines S at a time t just in case a theoretically complete description of P at t can be extended in one and only one way to a theoretically complete description of S at t. For details on how to make such a principle more precise using the theory of models, see G. Hellman and F. Thompson, 'Physicalism: ontology, determination, and reduction', *Journal of*

Philosophy, LXXII (1975), pp. 551–641. Dynamically, P at t determines S at later t' if and only if a complete description of P at t is theoretically compatible with one and only one complete description of S at t'. Dynamic unique determination is incompatible with the Principle of Interdependence (since later s elements would be fixed by the base alone). The constraint (1) is intended to rule out both dynamic and static unique determination.

Throughout it is assumed that theoretically complete descriptions of the the base or superstructure would involve much abstraction, that not every detail is relevant. Without this assumption, the prospect of part of an interdependent system uniquely determining the whole appears not so outlandish. However, from this standpoint, the system could, like a hologram, just as plausibly be reconstructed from *any* substantial proper part, from the superstructure as well as the base. This is of no use to historical materialism, and directly violates the third adequacy condition imposed below.

11 The falsity of unique determination by the base was clearly recognized, if not in so many words, by Engels in his clarification of historical materialism as maintaining that the mode of production is 'decisive in the last instance' and that the various aspects of the superstructure 'have an impact on the course of historical struggles and in many cases chiefly determine their form.' [F. Engels, Letter to Joseph Bloch, in *Friedrich Engels Profile*, H. Hirsch (ed.) (Wuppertal 1970), pp. 272, 273; author's translation.] This, as well as Engels' examples, suggest that antecedent s conditions (for many events) cannot in general be further resolved into component b and s conditions, and so on back, with negligible s remainder. How 'decisive' may be construed compatible with our condition (1) will appear below.

12 Karl Marx, *loc. cit.*

13 See McMurtry, *op. cit.*, who frames a similar principle in terms of 'compliance'. He argues, rightly, I believe, that such a principle is no more vague than Darwin's formulation of the principle of natural selection. For further considerations on vagueness, see below, p. 153.

14 The ultimate grounding of such 'nomological necessity' is quite beyond the scope of this paper. The only claim being urged with regard to this problematic notion is that it applies in the social realm and is not restricted to the 'natural' less the social.

15 McMurtry, *op. cit.*, employs the term 'blocks' analogously.

16 It should be noted that special problems arise in any effort to count cases of incompatibility in the second sense, where kinds of alternatives are involved. A simple enumeration of predicates would surely be oversimplified. Rather the kinds must also be weighted according to some measure of importance. Thus, one cannot claim throughly to have met the second adequacy condition. What we have done, however, is sketched how blanket statements involving the 'overall importance' of base or superstructure may be replaced by more specific questions concerning the importance of kinds of

alternatives to existing conditions. Hopefully, these are more tractable questions.

17   Without minimizing the divergence in purposes and interests behind disputes over materialism, it is worth noting that to some extent disagreements over selection themselves stem from disagreements over the nature of social change. Thus, extensive concentration on the attitudes of 'great leaders' stems partly from the view that their wills have a greater impact than would be granted by most materialists.

18   The differential method applies to laws of form (6), but not necessarily to the most general laws that may exist. Thus, there may be general laws of form

$$(6')\qquad\qquad C(b,s,t) \rightarrow C'(b,s,t'),$$

taking a complete state of the system in b and s variables at a time to a complete state at another time. It might be thought that differential methods could be employed to measure the extent of change in the system so described at t' produced by b and s variables respectively. However, when the resultant is complex, as in $(6')$, severe problems of heterogeneity arise. How does one compare different sets of changes along several parameters at once, when there is no evident way of weighting the parameters? My approach avoids this by working only with resultants, r, that have metrics, considering them one at a time in laws of form (6). Imprecision is then shifted to the selection of historically important resultants. This shift at least allows the theory to get off the ground.

19   J. S. Mill, *A System of Logic* (London 1961), bk. 3, ch. 8; bk. 6, ch. 7, sec. 3.

20   The Principle of Interdependence merely asserts that any substantial variation in a b (s) variable requires (as cause) variation of some s (b) variable. Obviously this is compatible with variation of many sets of $b(s)$ variables independent of variation of many sets of $s(b)$ variables.

21   See Herbert A. Simon, *The Sciences of the Artificial* (Cambridge Mass. 1969), ch. 4.

22   See the parallel remarks above (at the end of the third section) concerning selection and weighting with respect to dialectical base predominance.

23   It should be noted that there still remain thorny problems of measurement in applying the differential method even in particular cases of a law of form (6) governing a single magnitude r.

In the simplest case, only two antecedent conditions would appear in a law of form (6), one from b and one from s:

$$b_1 \text{ and } s_1 \rightarrow r'.$$

Within this assumption, the simplest further assumption would be that, holding b_1 (s_1) approximately fixed, there is a unique change, $\Delta s_1(\Delta b_1)$, in the other factor affecting r, by $(\Delta r)b_1$ $((\Delta r)s_1)$, compatible with all laws governing the system. Then all that is needed to determine the relative weighting in the particular instance is to compare $(\Delta r)b_1$ with $(\Delta r)s_1$. Of course, this uniqueness assumption cannot generally be made. Generally a range of variation of one factor will be compatible with near fixity of the other. The natural course then is to compare the maximum total changes in r across the whole range of variation in first one, then the other, factor permitted by the laws on the relevant fixity assumptions. Comparison of the maximum changes, max $(\Delta r)b_1$ and max $(\Delta r)s_1$, settles the relative weighting of b_1 and s_1 in the particular instance.

In more complex cases, different changes in r can result from different variations among several combinations of factors within b or s. In some instances, it will be clear how to compare maximum changes; but in others comparison would be problematic since one may insist on taking into account 'how much' variation of antecedent conditions (permitted by the laws) would produce the change in the resultant. For example, does one want to count something as more susceptible to change from (say) s than b merely because in fact greater variation of s variables is compatible with near fixity of b variables than *vice versa*? I know of no generally satisfactory solution to this problem.

If you would like to receive regular news on Harvester Press publications, please just send your name and address to our Publicity Department, The Harvester Press Ltd., 17 Ship Street, Brighton, Sussex. We will then be pleased to send you our new announcements and catalogues and special notices of publications in your fields of interest.